animation:
the art
and the
industry

the art & design series

For beginners, students, and professionals in both fine and commercial arts, these books offer practical how-to introductions to a variety of areas in contemporary art and design.

Each illustrated volume is written by a working artist, a specialist in his or her field, and each concentrates on an individual area—from advertising layout or printmaking to interior design, painting, and cartooning, among others. Each contains information that artists will find useful in the studio, in the classroom, and in the marketplace.

Some of the books in the series:

susan rubin is a filmmaker and producer who teaches courses on animation. She is Vice President of Product Planning at Interactive Picture Systems, Inc., in New York City, where she works on software development for computer educational, and entertainment.

She has designed and directed her own award-winning animated films and has worked extensively as a producer of animation and special effects for television commercials.

ANIMATION

the art
and
the industry

susan rubin

illustrated by
susan rubin and joey ahlbum

A SPECTRUM BOOK

Prentice-Hall, Inc.
Englewood Cliffs, N.J. 07632

Library of Congress Cataloging in Publication Data

Rubin, Susan.
    Animation, the art and the industry.

    (The Art & design series)
    "A Spectrum Book."
    Bibliography:
    Includes index.
    1. Animation (Cinematography) I. Title. II. Series.
TR897.5.R8 1984   778.5'347   84-8333
ISBN 0-13-037797-X
ISBN 0-13-037789-9 (pbk.)

The Art & Design Series

© 1984 by Prentice-Hall, Inc.,
Englewood Cliffs, New Jersey 07632

A SPECTRUM BOOK

10 9 8 7 6 5 4 3 2 1

Printed in the United States of America
Book design and layout by Maria Carella
Manufacturing buyers: Edward J. Ellis
and Doreen Cavallo
Cover design by Hal Siegel
Production supervision by Inkwell
Technical advisor to the author: Howard Danelowitz

ISBN 0-13-037797-X

ISBN 0-13-037789-9 {PBK.}

Prentice-Hall International, Inc., London
Prentice-Hall of Australia Pty. Limited, Sydney
Prentice-Hall Canada Inc., Toronto
Prentice-Hall of India Private Limited, New Delhi
Prentice-Hall of Japan, Inc., Tokyo
Prentice-Hall of Southeast Asia Pte. Ltd., Singapore
Whitehall Books Limited, Wellington, New Zealand
Editora Prentice-Hall do Brasil Ltda., Rio de Janeiro

contents

preface

My motivation for writing this book is my love for animation and my fascination with its vast and varied potential for expression, communication, and creativity. It is essentially this that I hope to pass on to its readers, together with an explanation of the basic technical possibilities available in working with the medium.

I'll discuss the numerous career possibilities for those interested in working professionally in animation. The animation industry offers a multitude of positions for many specialized skills. This book intends to acquaint those readers interested in the applications of animation with the wide range of opportunities available to them, and to explore the commercial roles involved in the animation business.

The selection of interviews of people who work in the animation field provides the reader with first-hand insights into their personal impressions, experiences, and reactions as they discuss their careers.

For every question answered in this book, another is raised. It is my intention to challenge, provoke, and inspire the reader to discover and create the answers to these questions, and thereby to mold and stretch the medium to its full potential.

The use of the pronouns "he" and "his" throughout the book is a choice of convenience in writing style made consciously by the author, as constant use of "he or she" and "his or her" becomes awkward. It is essential to point out that both women and men are included in all discussions, and are involved in all aspects of the animation industry.

I would like to acknowledge the following people:

for reading my manuscript and offering invaluable suggestions and guidance: my parents Selma and Bernard Rubin, my brother Eric Rubin, and my long-time friend and mentor Eric Martin;

for contributing his skill, talent, and time in

joining me in the creation of the illustration and design of the book: Joey Ahlbum;

for working with me to expand and improve Chapter 2: Howard Danelowitz, Joseph Freeman, and Boris Bode;

for sharing their experiences: all of the people whom I interviewed for the book;

for assisting me editorially and answering my ongoing questions: my editor Mary Kennan;

and for offering me advice, moral support, friendship, and love, without which I could not have completed this project: Wendy Richmond, Jane Dickson, Harold Friedman, Doros, Jill Taffet, Danny and Liz, David Rubin, and of course, Paul Hodara.

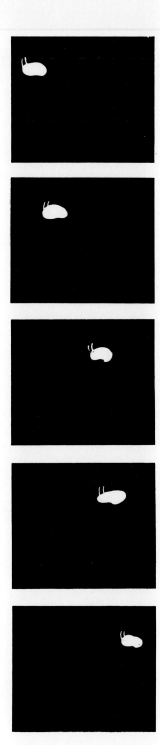

for my parents

introduction

The foundation of animation is illusion: the illusion of movement through picture change. Whether we are perceiving twelve progressing positions of a bird in flight through a spinning zoetrope toy, flipping through the successively drawn pages of a flip book, watching Mickey Mouse run across the movie screen, seeing a face metamorphose into a car, or viewing a calculator floating gracefully through a starry night in a television commercial, we are essentially being confronted by the results of rapidly changing sequential still images. Animation is made possible by the way we perceive a series of images. The ability of our retina to retain a visual image for approximately one-tenth of a second is called persistence of vision. It is this trait that allows us to see a credible illusion of continuity in a rapid succession of still images. The conceptual equivalent of persistence of vision is known as the phi phenomenon, which enables us to understand these successive images as connected and related. These two characteristics of our visual perception make it possible for us to read a series of rapidly changing images as one image in the process of plastic change, and for us to believe that we are seeing what we know to be fantastic or impossible. Suppose, for example, a hand is photographed frame by frame as it moves toward, behind, and away from an arm in small increments. With proper choreography and accurate timing, the hand, when projected, will appear to slice right through the arm.

From the caveman's early paintings and the Greek vases and friezes that portrayed images of stages of motion, man has been intrigued by the graphic representation of movement. The medium of animation existed before the advent of celluloid film and is moving rapidly beyond film into the realm of the computer. Our fascination with the illusion of movement persists, and we constantly explore current modes of motion synthesis to objectify it.

The cornerstone of animation is the rapid substitution of one still image by the next. From this base, the possibilities are limitless. Stories can be told; concepts can be explained; textures can be created and changed; visual poems can be related; products can be sold; three-dimensional objects can appear to move. The content of the whole sequence, as well as each and every image used to create it, is the choice of the animation designer. Indeed, the definition of the infinitive <u>to animate</u> is "to impart life to," and its boundaries are defined only by imagination and ingenuity.

Since its beginnings, there has always been a demand for animation, and the field has grown to become a dynamic and expanding commercial industry.

From the earliest cartoons, animation has been a form of popular entertainment for both children and adults. Animated shorts accompanied feature film presentations in the theaters. Saturday morning television cartoon series continue to mesmerize children. Animated features are released and rereleased.

Animation is used to explain and illustrate concepts in educational and industrial films. Sometimes this is because of its graphic clarity. Sometimes it can portray what cannot be seen otherwise. Sometimes it is considered to be a more accessible teaching tool.

The advertising business regularly uses animation in its television commercials. Cartoon characters may enact a 30-second story to sell a product. Graphic animation may highlight and dramatize a logo or tag line. A computer-generated environment may be the backdrop for a product demonstration or sales pitch. In fact, it is often the money spent by advertisers that is used to expand and refine the technologies and design capabilities of the animation medium.

You may choose to direct your energy and ability toward animation as an art form, free from the demands of clients and the restraints and rituals of commercialism. Or you may elect to enter the animation industry, where you will be paid to adapt your talents to the needs of your clients, and where the numerous functions required to create an animated film are marketable skills.

the
methods

4

The starting point in animation is the idea. The vast range of aesthetics and techniques selected to objectify that idea is the choice of the animator. For each new idea, a new choice of tools can be made in order to discover the most satisfactory and elegant means of expression.

Animation deals with movement. To begin, we look to scientific reality, to the physical properties of materials such as weight, volume, gravity, elasticity, and speed, and to Sir Isaac Newton's (1642–1727) laws of physical motion. The first law states that a body at rest will remain at rest and a body in motion will remain in motion in a straight line, unless it is compelled to change that state by forces impressed on it. The second law states that a force exerted on a body will cause the body to accelerate. The third states that for every force there is an equal and opposite reaction.

The animator may play with, and even contradict, all these elements of reality. Take, for instance, the simple example of a bouncing ball. What is the ball made of? How big is it? How much does it weigh? How fast is it traveling? What happens to it when it hits the ground? Perhaps it's an ordinary pink rubber ball, that weighs a quarter of a pound and simply bounces back up when it hits the ground. In animation, there are infinite options for this ball's activity, controlled in each drawing of each new frame. Perhaps it is indeed an ordinary pink rubber ball. But perhaps it falls very slowly like a feather and changes colors as it does. Maybe it falls right through the ground. Maybe it transforms into a bird in midair and flies away. Or it could hit the ground, pause, then suddenly take off very quickly in the opposite direction. It could even smash into little pieces upon impact, like glass.

A number of concepts are used frequently by animators to create the gestures and movements they desire. One commonly used to give a feeling of weight in a character is known as squash and stretch. Using this type of animation, a character or object will have a plasticity rather than the rigidity of a cement block. A bouncing ball provides a good illustration of this kind of elasticity. As a ball falls to the ground, it stretches; at the moment it hits the earth, it recoils and becomes squashed. In another example, a character may fall over a cliff, get caught on an outstretched tree limb, and be flung all the way back up to the top of the cliff again. As these actions occur, the character's body will be stretched and squashed accordingly.

1.1 Exaggerated gestures and movement illustrate anticipation and overlapping action.

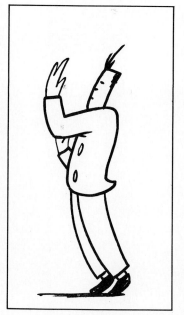

1.2

Anticipation and overlapping action are two other concepts that often enhance the power of the animation. Anticipation is the small preliminary action that leads in to the major action. When animating a character from one position to another, it can be more convincing on screen to animate her moving in the opposite direction first, just as a golfer has a large backswing before following through to hit the ball. This opposing preliminary motion is known as "anticipation."

Overlapping action refers to the movement of different parts of a character's body, clothing, and accessories at different rates of speed, which all relate to the main activity. Overlapping action is a common way of increasing the drama and emotion of the animation. (See Figure 1.1.)

In short, the possibilities are endless. The animator must determine the rules of the reality chosen and adhere to or break these rules as necessary.

Walt Disney was a master of animated gags. His humor lies in the unexpected and implausible events that occur by breaking the rules of a reasonable environment. Let us look for a moment at his film Steamboat Willie. Made in 1928, it was his third Mickey Mouse cartoon and the first to have musical accompaniment. The story is a simple one, taking place on a riverboat. It involves Peg Leg Pete, Mickey, and Minnie, and it is essentially a vehicle for the high point of the cartoon, in which he "plays" "Turkey in the Straw," using the domestic animals on the boat as if they were musical instruments. Certain rules of this cartoon reality are established and easily accepted because they are derived from our own reality. For example, the relative movement of objects defines their space and position. Everything has its proper gravity, solidity, and weight. When Mickey walks behind a wall, he is no longer visible due to the

1.2 Peg Leg Pete and Mickey Mouse confront each other in "Steamboat Willie."
Copyright © 1928, Walt Disney Productions.

5

suggested existence of the wall. When he grasps the steering wheel, it remains solidly there. And when Peg Leg Pete kicks Mickey down the stairs, he falls to the floor below, according to an exaggerated version of the laws of physics. When Mickey falls into a pail of water, the set of drawings that comprise the sequence emphasizes the step-by-step downward movement involved in falling. It is not merely a conventional uniform motion; rather, the weight of Mickey's belly pulls it down as his arms and legs fly up to counterbalance him. This is called <u>secondary motion</u>, and its result is a strongly empathic credibility.

An extension of this cause and effect relationship is the scene in which Mickey tries to salvage Minnie's guitar from a goat's mouth. He grabs it and pulls, and the goat pulls back, creating a comic tug-o-war. Again, the technical execution of the scene increases its realism. Both Mickey's feet and the goat's feet are solidly planted on the ground. The stretching back of their bodies, contrasting the firm positioning of their feet, emphasizes the opposing pulls.

Conventional reactions reinforce the credibility of this world—objects cast shadows, the boat leaves a wake, sounds accompany actions in a reasonable manner. Having established certain rules, Disney proceeds to break others, through the "impossible" distortions and "unrealistic" events possible in animation. For all the reassuring realism of locale and essential plot, Disney's intention in <u>Steamboat Willie</u> is to send us into a new universe with new rules, defined by a careful trade-off of familiar and unfamiliar elements.

Mickey is designed to move easily and credibly, so that the "incredible" incidents he is involved in are acceptable. For example, when Peg Leg Pete yanks Mickey toward him in anger, instead of pulling him closer, he stretches Mickey's stomach like a rubber band that flops onto the floor before Mickey can tuck it all back into his pants. The plausible facial expressions of each character and the interruption of gravity as the deformed stomach drops onto the floor force us to accept this implausible sequence.

The same concepts apply to Peg Leg Pete's chewing tobacco. To allow him to spit, his two front teeth slide open and then slam shut again. The fact that the rest of the scene is serene and credible—the background moves on by, and Peg Leg Pete responds in expected fashion as the tobacco juice flies back with the wind, first hitting the bell, then hitting him in the face—increases the impact of the incredibility of Peg Leg Pete's teeth.

This tension between expected and unexpected, reality and fantasy, contributes to the magic of animation, with its own laws and events.

To be able to create and explore this territory of the imagination, we must have a grasp of the tools of animation that are available to us.

animation tools

The graphic power of animation lies not in a single complex image, as it does in a painting, etching, or photograph. Rather, it is in a succession of rapidly changing images. Artwork is created for each frame. It is then conventionally photographed by an animation camera frame by frame, and later projected at twenty-four frames per second. There are, however, several forms of cameraless animation. One such method is the use of sprocketed film leader. Leader is plastic film stock, with sprocket holes along the edges for camera and projector threading, that has no image or frame lines on it. It may be purchased in black, clear, and colors, and is generally used on the heads and tails of films to lead in and out of the picture. To create animation, black leader can be punched with holes of different sizes and shapes. The emulsion can be scratched off with a sharp instrument in various patterns, and then dyed in colors. When the leader is projected, it creates exciting animated rhythms and forms where the light passes through it. (See Figure 1.3.)

It is also possible to draw directly onto clear film leader or already existing live-action footage. Different color inks and paints can be used to

draw images frame by frame, or to color in whole areas of the film. Letraset or other such material can be adhered to clear leader to create unusual textures when the leader is projected. Sounds can be made by using single-perforated clear leader and marking on the area along the edge of the film that travels over the sound head of the projector. (See Figure 1.4.)

A wonderful form of cameraless animation is the flip book, which is a stack of separate images flipped by hand to create the illusion of movement or transformation. A flip book is a good way to begin to animate. It is simple, inexpensive, and very portable. You need only a stack of paper and a pen. A small notepad works well, or a pile of blank index cards. Each new drawing is made by aligning the new page over the last, and tracing through for reference and registration, making the necessary changes from one drawing to the next. A lightbox, a translucent drawing surface with a light source under it, may be useful to make it easier to see through to the preceding image. When all the drawings have been completed, the pages are bound together at one end by a clip, staples, tape, or any other desired binding, and flipped through at the desired speed. A flip book can also be filmed and projected. The flip book is one of the most basic ways of creating animation. It can be used to make sketches of larger ideas for films, to study and test specific types of movements, or to illustrate a short story or simple idea as a final product in itself.

One of the first creative options facing the animator is the technique in which the artwork will be created. Often, it is drawn frame by frame onto paper. A simple pencil may be used, but drawing instruments may include colored pens, paint and paint brushes, magic markers, crayons, pastels, and charcoal. Or perhaps the images will be created with rubber stamps, col-

1.3 Scratched and punched 35 mm black leader.

1.4 Drawing frame by frame on 35 mm clear leader.

7

1.3

1.4

8 lage elements, or adhesive labels. These choices are determined by the kinds of images desired, whether they are realistic character drawings or abstract patterns of color and texture.

And on what material will the drawings be made? Perhaps the choice will be white paper. Perhaps it will be different colored sheets of paper, pieces of newspaper, or corrugated cardboard. Transparent cellulose acetate, known as "cel," may be used to create several layers of animation artwork. Thus, the animation in a scene can be broken down into component parts on each layer of cel and recomposited under the camera during the filming process to provide for greater flexibility and control in the creation of the sequence. Frosted cel is also available. It is translucent to allow for layers of artwork, but its surface accepts pencil and crayon in addition to the adhesive vinyl cel paint commonly used with clear acetate cels. A more detailed discussion of cel animation follows in the next section.

Animation artwork may be created using underlit materials. Silhouetted coins, matches, or cutout forms can be moved on a backlit tabletop while being filmed frame by frame. Piles of sand or smears of ink and paint can be lit from underneath and manipulated and changed frame by frame. Kodalith film and colored gels can also be used. A Kodalith is artwork made on high contrast film. (See Figures 1.7 and 1.8.) The image itself is clear, and the rest of the frame is black. A gel is a transparent colored sheet of acetate. By combining Kodaliths and various gels and lighting them from underneath, a unique style of graphic animation is produced.

1.5

1.6

1.7

1.8

1.5 Photograph and rubber stamps.

1.6 Photograph and Letraset.

1.7 Negative Kodalith

1.8 Positive Kodalith

1.9 Photograph, Letraset, and spray paint.

1.9

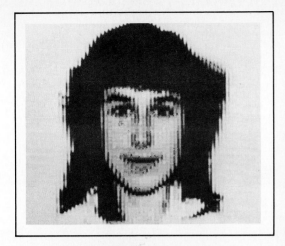

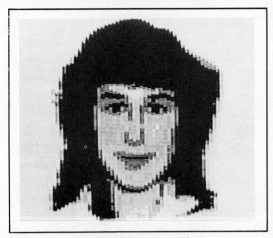

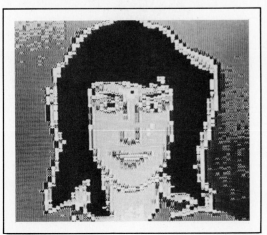

Any three-dimensional object may be animated in any way imaginable by simply moving it by small increments and filming it frame by frame. A whole sink full of dirty dishes can miraculously wash and stack itself with no apparent human intervention.

Already-existing imagery, such as photographs or illustrations, may be used as raw material. They can be cut up, altered, and moved around. They can be combined with drawn or painted artwork to create collaged effects.

Computers also create imagery for animation. Some computers allow for the manipulation and distortion of existing artwork. Other computers generate two and three dimensional images, and animate them as well.

The selection of graphic material and technique should support and further the idea for the film and the look the animator wishes to achieve in expressing this idea. Each method of working results in its own feeling. Sometimes, only through experimentation, testing, and an open mind, will the best approach be revealed. Because each frame of film is created separately, combinations of several methods may be desired. Before we investigate more closely the techniques of working in any of these media, it is important to point out that the restraints on such choices are only the limits of invention of the animator. He may elect to work in a conventional drawing style to communicate his idea. He may, though, avail himself of the wide range of graphic combinations to achieve his final product. (See Figure 1.12.)

1.10 Video-scanned photo converted into low-resolution microcomputer display.

1.11 The "Light Cycles" from "TRON." Three-dimensional, high-resolution, light-sourced raster graphics composed of geometric solids. Produced by Magi-Synthavision. Copyright 1982, Walt Disney Productions.

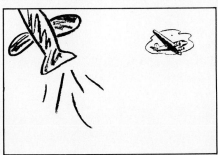

1.13

drawn animation

In drawn animation, each drawing changes from the one preceding it to create a flow of images. The way the drawings change, and the amount of variation from one drawing to the next, is determined by what is being animated and the speed and feeling of the movement. The more subtle the change, the more fluid the animation will appear. More drastic changes from drawing to drawing will create faster, more abrupt movement.

Let us examine a simple illustration. Suppose we wish to animate a leaf falling from a tree to the ground in two seconds. Since the film will be projected at 24 frames per second, we have 48 frames in which to move the line. Often, due to the nature of drawing small increments of change, animation works best when each drawing is shot for two frames. In this case, we will need 24 drawings to make the leaf travel from the tree to the ground. In certain cases, it is more appropriate to shoot each drawing only once, for instance when moving a line from the top to the bottom of a page very smoothly. In this case we would need 48 drawings of the line. Movements from north to south or from east to west are known as "panning movements." Unless they are animated using one frame per drawing, they can create a strobing effect when projected. Unless this is desirable, panning movements should be animated "on ones." In other cases it is possible to shoot each drawing for three or maybe four frames. In these cases, we would need, respectively, 16 or 12 drawings of the line. In such cases our movement would look more staccato, or jumpy, as we increase the amount of frames taken of each drawing. The proper number of frames for each drawing is determined by the type of movement desired. Shooting 48 drawings frame by frame will result

1.13 Drawing and rubber stamp.

in a much smoother motion than shooting 12 drawings at four frames each. Eventually, an animator may develop a feeling for the number of drawings he needs for a specific sequence of movement. However, it is often necessary before a final decision can be made to shoot a preliminary motion test, known as a pencil test, in order to actually see how the movement will work at different rates of shooting. (See Figure 1.14.)

Registration is the technique of assuring that corresponding points on two sequential frames bear the correct relationship to each other. It is an urgent consideration that the drawings remain in registration with each other when they are being drawn as well as when they are being shot. When using index cards or heavier paper, it is possible to keep the drawings registered by making sure the edges and corners are always lined up from one drawing to the next. But this can be difficult with normal weight paper and requires constant attention. The standard registration system uses three holes punched either along the top or the bottom of each sheet of paper. These holes correspond to three pegs on a pegbar onto which the punched paper is placed. (See Figure 1.15.) Animators will often bottom peg their drawings, as it comfortably allows them to place their fingers between the drawings and "flip" them back and forth to examine the movement. The holes and the pegs are, of course, outside of the field of artwork that the camera will shoot. There are two standard patterns of holes, which are very similar. They are Oxberry punch and Acme punch. Both consist of two rectangular holes with a circular hole in the middle. All drawings are made with the punched paper lined up on the pegbar. There is a matching pegbar on the animation stand, so that the drawings can be aligned precisely as they were drawn when they are being shot.

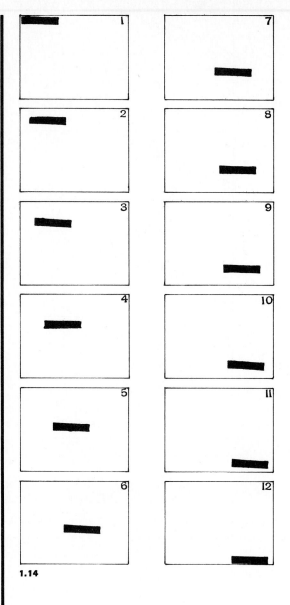

1.14

1.14 A line animates from the top to the bottom of the frame in 12 drawings. If each image were shot for two frames, the sequence would last one second when projected.

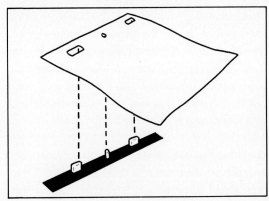

1.15

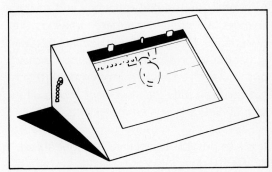

1.16

Other systems of registration can be devised, using, for instance, a standard three-hole notebook punch, or a right-angled wedge to hold the corners of the paper when drawing and when shooting. But it must be understood that the ability to control the animation depends partially on carefully registered drawings.

The registration and animation of the drawings are made easier by working on a light table. A new drawing is made by placing the paper over the previous drawing. The light table enables the animator to see through the drawing he or she is working on to the drawing underneath, to use it as reference and to trace any areas he or she intends to remain the same. The light table gives the animator a clear reference of what previous drawings have been, and how they have changed, aiding in the creation of each new drawing added to the sequence.

A light table can be either purchased or built. Its essential elements are a translucent drawing surface with a light source underneath. A simple homemade lightbox can be made using an empty wooden drawer with a lightbulb inside and a piece of frosted Plexiglass laid over it. The drawing surface should be at a comfortable height for drawing. If possible, a fluorescent bulb should be used because it is a much cooler light source than a standard tungsten lightbulb. A professional animation table has a rotating circular translucent glass disk inserted into a mechanical drawing table. The angle of the table top, as well as of the circular drawing disk, can be adjusted for maximum drawing comfort. There is a built-in light source below the glass disk and a standard registration pegbar along the top of it. (See Figure 1.16.)

It is very important that drawings be numbered as they are drawn, so their order can be easily reestablished. Each drawing may be very similar

1.15 Animation pegbar and punched paper.

1.16 Homemade lightbox with angled drawing surface, lit from behind by lightbulb. Drawings are registered by the pegbar along the top edge of the light table.

14

to those around it, so it can become confusing if they are not numbered. Any other notes can be made in the margins of the drawings, indicating holds, reverses, and other instructions, so that all actions intended when drawing will not be overlooked during the shooting. Coding may be used to separate one sequence from another. Because there are such large quantities of drawings made for an animated film, it is useful to create a simple system of organization to avoid careless errors and confusion.

When beginning to animate, map out a "path of action" with a simple line. This is the line of movement that your character will follow. Rough out your drawings, and once the basic construction of the animation is complete, make sure your lines of action are well conceived. The line of action is the imaginary line extending from the top to the bottom of the animated character or object, highlighting its gesture and position in the movement. After the basic action is sketched out, go back and clean up the drawings and add the details. At this stage, think about using exaggeration and unusual perspective to heighten the scene. Begin loosely, as your drawings will reflect your liveliness and spontaneity.

Drawn animation can also be done from "pose to pose" drawings. These are the initial pictures exemplifying how you visualize the character or object to be animated. In character animation,

these drawings are used to make "model sheets" that display the physical appearance of the character in different positions. You can use these drawings to guide you. Start with the first pose of your movement, and then find your next position. A pose is known as a hold, an extreme, or a key drawing. (See Figure 1.17.)

The drawings that fill in the motion between the extreme position are called "in-betweens." The number of in-betweens is determined by the length of time it takes to get from one position to another. Any speed variations and rhythm changes are created as these drawings are being made. The advantage in working this way is that the action can be predetermined and laid out. However, be aware that preplanning that is too rigid can stifle the movement and result in stiff, unnatural animated movements.

It is also possible to animate "straight ahead." That is, the direction of the animation evolves as it progresses. There may not be a known end to the film, but as the drawings transform and metamorphose from one to the next, a film develops and wends its way along. This method can be very spontaneous and natural. Its biggest drawback is that an animator may find he has gone in an unsuitable direction. Particularly if a model sheet has not been used, the character or object can evolve in an undesirable way.

The use of drawn cycles may be helpful to the

1.17 Key drawings 1, 5, 10.

animator. A cycle is a series of drawings that repeat. Some cycles begin and end with the same position. By designing such a cycle, the same set of drawings can be used repeatedly as needed. An example of this is an animated rainstorm, in which the falling raindrops are a continuous cycle of eight to ten drawings, which appear to be an endless downpour. (See Figure 1.18.)

Drawn animation may be filmed either toplit or backlit. If it is lit from behind, interesting and unexpected textures may result when the film is projected because of the grain of the paper and the line quality being used.

Whether drawing from pose to pose, straight ahead, or a combination of both, timing is the crucial consideration. It refers to how the animator varies the changes in actions within a scene. No matter how well the animator is drawing, if the pictures are not paced out properly, none of the animation will look convincing. Timing is the essence of the art of animation and usually takes a while to master.

cel animation

Cel animation refers to the use of one or more layers of transparent sheets onto which animation drawings have been transferred, and which are filmed to produce a desired kinetic effect. The use of cels allows for far more complex imagery and activity than would be possible if every element of the drawing had to be recreated for each new frame, as in drawn animation. When only part of a drawing is to be animated and the rest of it remains constant, it is not necessary to redraw the whole drawing frame by frame. By drawing on several layers of transparent acetate, separate elements of a scene may be animated on separate levels of cels. For example, suppose that we wish to animate a man walking along a river as it begins to rain. The background scene can be created as a piece of static artwork. The man can then be animated walking on a series of transparent

1.18 Eight-frame cycle: Drawing 1 and drawing 9 are the same.

cells overlaid on the background scene. The rainstorm can be animated on a third layer of cels and laid on top of the man and river when it begins to rain. When filming this sequence, the cel levels are composited, and each cel level is changed accordingly for every frame. On the screen, the image appears as a single level of action.

The name <u>cel</u> comes from the original celluloid plastic sheets that were used. These were made from a tough, but highly flammable plastic, which has now been replaced by cellulose acetate, but they are still referred to as cels. Generally, animation cels are 10.5 inches by 13 inches, and 0.005 inches thick. They can be bought in quantity, already punched with either Oxberry or Acme registration holes. Registration is quite important in working with cels, especially because different parts of each image are on different layers of cel, which must be carefully and accurately registered to each other.

Numbering systems for artwork are more complex and specific in cel animation. Each sequence may have more than one series of drawings in it. These drawings must not only remain in order, but also stay in exact correspondence to the other drawings with which they will be combined in shooting. Each cel should be identified with an indication of what sequence it is part of, what number drawing it is in the sequence, and what layer it is on. A combination of numbers and letters may be helpful in identifying cels.

The clear identification of each cel is even more important if a cameraman shoots the artwork for the animator. The animator must create exposure sheets, detailed instructions for the cameraman as to how the artwork should be shot. An exposure sheet keeps a record of anywhere from 64 to 96 frames of film. There are separate columns for the background(s) and up to four cel levels. They account for every layer of artwork for every frame. In addition, there are columns for noting the occurrence of dialogue, descriptions of action, and special camera instructions. The cameraman depends on the exposure sheets to indicate all changes in art-

work and camera position for every frame. Thus, each cel must be clearly identifiable so he or she will be able to follow instructions with as little error and confusion as possible. (See Figure 2.12 in the section entitled "Shooting the Animation.)

A great many cartoons and animated feature films have been made using cel animation, and the animation studios have developed a successful system for this technique.

Once the preliminary action has been sketched out, or "storyboarded" (See Figure 1.19), and the characters have been designed, the animation is drawn with pencil on punched paper. Each drawing is marked as to which elements will go on which cel levels. This animation is shot in what is known as a <u>pencil test</u>. The pencil test is screened, and the animation is adjusted until it is satisfactory.

Then, using lightweight animation gloves to protect the cels from fingerprints, the pencil drawings are traced with ink onto punched cels and broken down into separate layers. This step is known as <u>inking</u>. Today pencil drawings are often transferred onto cels by Xeroxing. As this technique becomes more refined, there is greater potential for more variation in color and line quality.

Next, the cels are painted. Special paints have been created to adhere to acetate without cracking or flaking. They are made from a water-based vinyl acrylic copolymer, and the most commonly used are manufactured by Cartoon Colour in Culver City, California. In a process known as <u>opaquing</u>, the paint is applied to the back side of the cels, one color at a time, by gently pushing a brush heavily loaded with paint right up to the middle of the inked lines. The paint should be applied barely touching the cel to avoid the occurrence of brushstrokes. Painting begins with the darker colors, starting from the middle of the object and working outward to the outline. As one progresses to the lighter colors, any color overlaps that may occur will not be seen by the camera.

The paint is applied after adding droplets of water to it. Water will evaporate from the paint

1 BOY IS STANDING ALONE SINGING A SONG.

2 CUT TO SNEAKER WALKING RIGHT TO LEFT.

3 SNEAKER APPROACHES BOY. BOY STOPS SINGING AND SHUFFLES NERVOUSLY.

4 BATTLE BETWEEN BOY AND SNEAKER.

5 BATTLE ENDS IN A DRAW. THEY BECOME THE BEST OF FRIENDS.

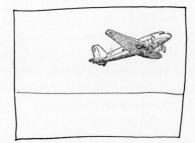

6 CUT TO AIRPLANE AS THEY FLY OFF INTO THE SUNSET.

1.19 Storyboard for a short narrative sequence.

18 mixture and should be added as necessary. The mixture should be stirred and the brush dipped into it. When the paint is just ready to drop off the brush, but clings instead, the consistency is correct. At this point the color should spread evenly without becoming too thin.

Each area of color must dry before the color next to it is applied. (See Figure 1.20.) Airbrushed textures and inked details can then be added to the front of the cels to enhance the drawings if desired. Once the cels are painted, they are ready to be shot onto film.

Many things can be achieved with cel animation that cannot be done with any other technique. However, it is a laborious, time-consuming, and expensive method of animating, and it has its own set of problems that are discussed in the following several paragraphs.

A layer of cel has a small but significant optical density that results in a slight darkening of what is underneath it. More than four or five layers of cel will severely decrease the vividness of the colors, unless the cel is a very thin weight, and even in this case, only one or two more layers are acceptable. Any change in the number of cels over the background will be perceptible when projected. Thus, the number of layers must remain constant throughout a scene, even if some are just blank cel levels. In addition, if a color on layer one near the background is supposed to be identical to a color on top, say, layer four, the color difference from one layer to the next must be compensated for during the painting stage. If the same color paint were used on both levels, the colors would appear to be slightly different in the final film. Placing cels over a color not only darkens it, but reduces its intensity as well. For this reason, the top color must be mixed with gray so that it will be seen correctly in relation to the bottom cel. If we were

1.20

1.20 At top is inked animation cel. Center shows painted animation cel: Paint is applied to the back side of the cel. At bottom is back side of painted cel.

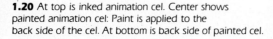

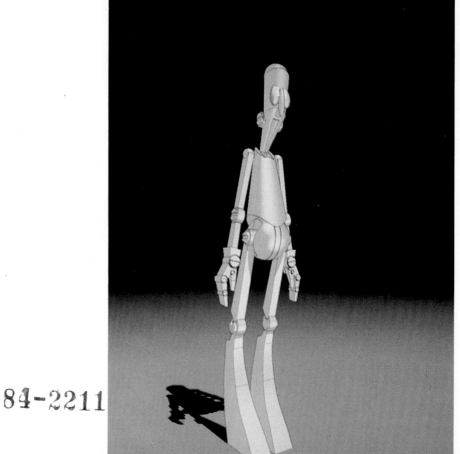

Plate 1
'Volcano'
Production: Computer Creations of New York
Client: WGGL-FM/Cleveland
Two-dimensional digital computer graphics

Plate 2
'Robot'
Production: MAGI–Synthavision
Designer: Chris Wedge
Three-dimensional raster graphics composed
of geometric solids

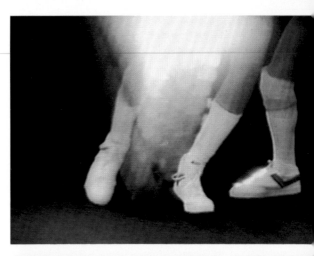

Plate 3
"Working Man"
Production: Robert Abel and Associates
Producer: Robert Abel
Director: Robert Abel
Designers/Animators: Maura Dutra, Randy
Roberts, Con Pederson
Technical Director: Jim Keating
Director of Photography: Laszlo Kovacs
Editor: Rick Ross
Client: Levi's
Three-dimensional computer animation
combined with live action

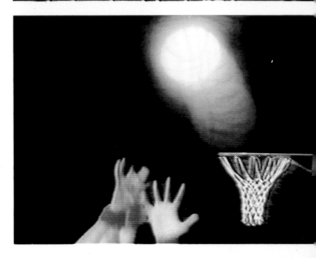

Plates 4 to 7
"Rebound"
Production: Dolphin Productions
Client: CBS
Analogue manipulation of live action

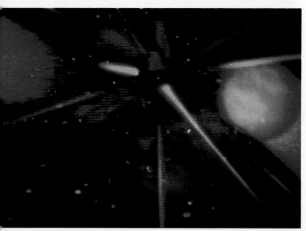

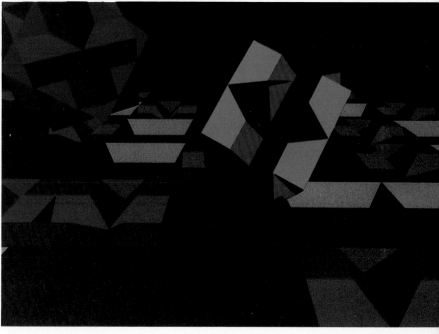

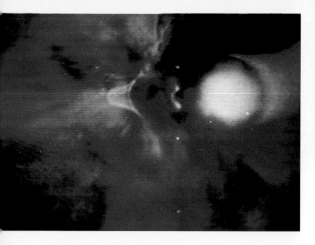

Plates 8 to 11
"Got Tu Go Disco"
Production: Dolphin Productions
Analogue computer graphics

Plate 12
"Merck Timoptol" beta-blocking molecules
Production: Digital Effects, Inc.
Designer: George Parker
Client: Romulus Productions
Three-dimensional solid,
light-sourced graphics

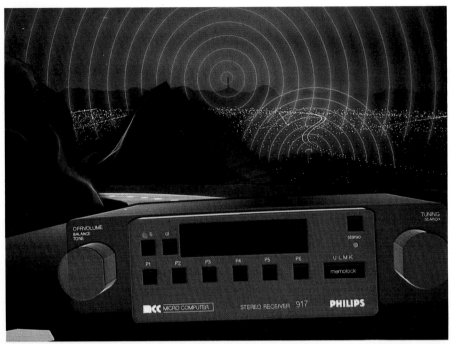

Plate 13
"Car Radio"
Production: Robert Abel and Associates
Producer: Robert Abel
Creative Director: Bill Kovacs
Technical Director: Bill Kovacs and
Steve Cooney
Client: Philips
Three-dimensional vector graphics

Plate 14
"Subway"
Production: Digital Effects, Inc.
Designer: Mark Lindquist
Two-dimensional digital paint
"Video Palette" system

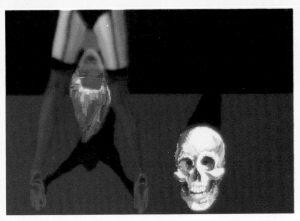

Plates 15 to 18
"Videodrome" trailer
Production: Harold Friedman Consortium, Ltd./
Digital Effects, Inc.
Designer: Mark Lindquist
Client: Creative Alliance, Inc./
Universal Pictures
Two-dimensional digital paint
"Video Palette" system

Plate 19
"Glider"
Production: Robert Abel and Associates
Producer: Robert Abel
Designer/Director: Randy Roberts
Technical Director: Richard Hollander
Camera Operator: John Nelson
Editor: Rick Ross
Model Photography: Tom Barron and
Tony Meininger
Client: Panasonic
Three-dimensional vector graphics

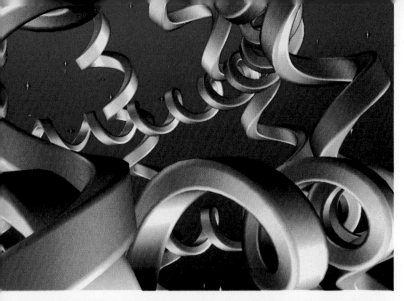

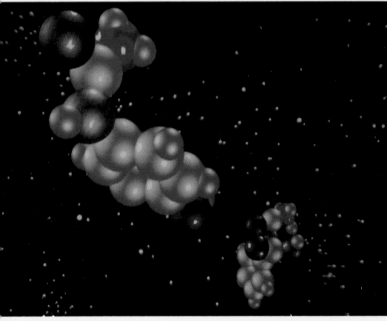

Plate 20 (top)
Production: Digital Effects, Inc.
Designer: George Parker
Client: N.W. Ayer/AT&T
Three-dimensional, light-sourced,
smooth-shaded, texture-mapping

Plate 21 (center)
"Bufferin" molecules
Production: Harold Friedman Consortium, Ltd./
MAGI–Synthavision
Three-dimensional light-sourced raster
graphics composed of geometric solids

Plate 22 (bottom)
"TRON"
Production: Robert Abel and Associates
Designer/Director: Kenny Mirman
Technical Director: Frank Vitz
Software and Technical Support: Bill Kovacs
Systems Supervisor: Robert Abel
Three-dimensional vector graphics
© 1982 Walt Disney Productions

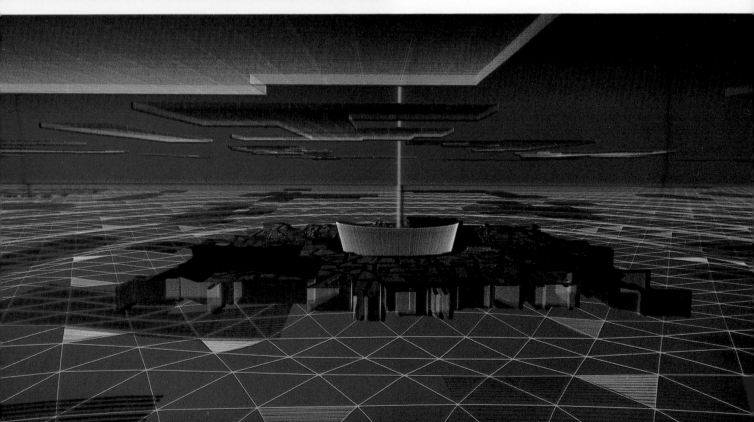

Plate 23
"Changing Pictures"
Production: Robert Abel and Associates
Executive Producer: Robert Abel
Designer/Director: Kenny Mirman
Technical Director: Frank Vitz
Assistant Technical Director: Richard Baily
Animation: Con Pederson and Jim Barrett
Producer: Bob Regalado
Client: TRW
Computer and cel animation combination

Plate 24
"Favorite Retreat"
Production: New York Institute
of Technology
Designer: Paul Xander, Sr.
Two-dimensional digital paint system
© NYIT

matching the bottom level color to the top level, we would have to add white to the bottom color. Graying colors is usually the preferable method when you are mixing your own colors. White is the most problematic color in cel levels. It is best to keep pure white on the bottom levels, as the top level white can be adjusted by adding gray, whereas if the pure white level were on top, we could not lighten the lower level whites to match it.

Commercially prepared cel paints come in base colors and color tints. These tints correspond directly to the gray scale, ranging from black to white, and may be used for cel compensation.

When matching colors, the animator should apply dabs of paint onto a cel, dry with a hair dryer, and compare colors under a bulb or quartz lamp that will emulate the same conditions under which the artwork will be filmed. He should also notice if the cel itself has a slight orange or blue cast to it. This may necessitate the addition of a small amount of another color when mixing for color compensation. Generally, it is preferable to use the clearest cels available.

A disadvantage of the cel method is that acetate reflects light into the camera lens. In addition, the glass platen that is placed over the cel layers to keep them flat also reflects light. Sometimes, a reflection of the camera itself will appear on the finished film. There are several ways to avoid this. Lights should be placed at no greater than a 45° angle to the artwork to avoid direct reflections into the lens. Polarizing filters can be used over the lights and the lens to cut unwanted glare. Exposure adjustments must be made when using polarizing filters. A black, non-reflecting cardboard matte can be attached underneath the camera, with a hole cut out for the lens to mask any reflections of the camera in the artwork.

Another problem is that of dust, which tends to cling to the acetate cels and the glass platen. Compressed air can be used to eliminate some unwanted dust from the cels, and the glass platen can be cleaned with a solution of ammo-

nia and water. Polarizing filters will minimize reflections from specks of dust on the cels. However, dust is a difficult problem to remedy, particularly when using dark backgrounds, and thus it is important to keep cels as clean as possible at all stages of the production.

It is suggested that cel animation be approached only after the beginning animator has had some experience with paper drawing animation, just as an artist learns to draw before attempting a more sophisticated rendering technique such as oil painting. The cel method tends to make any mistakes in the animation more obvious, as the dark lines and opaque colors appear to slow down the animation and make it heavier in appearance. Cel animation is costly compared to drawn animation, and too much of the beginner's time will be absorbed trying to master the cel process instead of concentrating on the drawings, pacing, and rhythm of the animation.

rotoscoping

Rotoscoping is the use of previously exposed film, such as live-action, as a reference standard for animation artwork. The live action is projected frame by frame, and drawings are made by tracing over areas of the live-action image. Rotoscoping offers the opportunity to create artwork that is in the subtle realm between the photographic and the drawn. The realistic image can be altered or enhanced depending on the choice of areas that are traced and the style in which the drawings are made. For example, in rotoscoping a live action scene of a bicycle rider riding through the city, the animator may trace only the bicycle wheels and the rider's feet and eliminate all other elements from the live action. He may then combine this rotoscoped image with an altogether abstract background.

Rotoscoping was developed by Max and Dave Fleischer, the creators of animated characters such as Betty Boop and Popeye, in New York in the early 1920s. They wanted to give their character Koko the Clown a credible movement as he lost his balance on a new pair of ice skates. So they filmed Dave Fleischer floundering on skates and used the live action image as reference for the animation by tracing him frame by frame and redrawing him as Koko.

Rotoscoping is also used to determine positioning for an animated element that will later be combined with live action. For example, if an animated laser is to beam into a live-action airplane, the live-action film must be shot first and traced frame by frame so that the placement of the laser beam can be determined. The artwork for each frame of the laser can then be created so that when it is shot and superimposed over the live action, the beam will, in fact, appear to hit the plane.

A necessary tool for rotoscoping is the capability to project the live action film frame by frame. Many projectors will not do this, and if a frame is held too long in the gate, it will melt from the heat of the projector lamp. There are, however, some projectors, such as the Athena 16mm, that will allow for single frame projection.

The animation camera, such as the Oxberry, can be adapted to project film down onto the table top below it frame by frame. The animator can trace the areas of the image as he or she desires.

A rotoscope setup can be arranged with a projector located underneath a drawing table that projects frame by frame onto a mirror which is angled at 45° to the drawing surface. The mirror throws the image up onto the rear side of a frosted glass table top. The animator can rotoscope this frame and advance the projector one frame at a time as he or she proceeds. (See Figure 1.22.)

The method described above is acceptable for drawings existing for their own sake. However, material that is rephotographed and composited with rotoscoped imagery would weave

1.21

1.21 Rotoscoping.

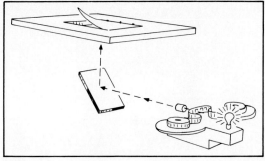

1.22

and jiggle if this technique were used. This is caused by the slight changes in alignment from one animation stand and camera to another. Any artwork produced by rotoscoping should be photographed through the same camera that was used to make it, to guarantee maximum alignment with the original film.

The simplest and most limited rotoscope setup is a single frame projector projecting onto a wall at a distance to make the image the desired size for the animation drawings. A pegbar is attached to the wall, and punched paper is hung vertically from it. The image is projected onto the paper and traced vertically. Each new frame is projected onto a clean sheet of paper. This system is suitable only if the drawing style is flexible enough so that the vertical position is not a major disadvantage.

If a single frame projector is not available, a photographic enlarger can be used as a rotoscope setup. The film holder would have to be adapted or rebuilt to hold the film comfortably, with a cutout opening the size of the film frame so that the image can be projected downward. The sprocket holes can be used as points of alignment.

A Xerox Copyflo machine can also be used as a rotoscope device. Using this method, the roll of film is copied onto a large roll of paper. The individual paper frames can then be cut and reregistered for tracing. Again, as with the enlarger technique, one can use the sprocket holes for registration and later mount each Xeroxed paper frame correspondingly on punched paper or cel.

direct animation
Direct animation refers to frame-by-frame animation that is achieved during the filming process. It is often known as animating "under the

1.22 An example of a rotoscope setup. The live-action film image is projected onto a mirror positioned at a 45° angle to the animation table top.
The film image is then reflected onto the translucent table top, where it can be traced and used as reference frame by frame as artwork is created.

21

camera," because the creation and manipulation from frame to frame occurs as the camera is shooting the film frame by frame.

One example of direct animation is filming a drawing frame by frame as it is gradually created on one piece of paper. When the film is projected, the drawing appears to grow on the screen. This same effect can be easily created by a series of drawings in which each new drawing adds a little to the drawing preceding it. The difference between the two is that animating a series of drawings prior to shooting enables preplanning and control of the progression of the animation, whereas animating the drawing under the camera allows for spontaneous, yet at the same time, irreversible decisions as to how the animation evolves. The selection of which method to use is up to the animator.

When direct animation is used to animate a three-dimensional object by moving it little by little, frame by frame, the process is called stop motion. The greater the distance the object is moved from frame to frame, the faster it appears to move when it is projected. The speed of movement of one object is also affected by the relative speed and positions of other objects in the frame.

Any object can be animated, from popcorn to toy cars to bits of colored glass. Paint may be smeared on glass in a gradual frame-by-frame metamorphosis. Similarly, pastels may be smudged on sanded paper to create animating forms frame by frame. Clusters of tiny beads or buttons can form patterns and changing shapes. Cutout images or shapes can be moved frame by frame as an animated interactive collage. It is helpful to use a small tool, such as tweezers or a toothpick, to facilitate the slight movement of small objects.

1.23 Object animation: single frame from a sequence of stop motion of a plastic airplane soaring through cotton ball clouds and toy stars.

Puppet animation is a form of direct animation that uses the art of puppetry to create animated puppet characters on film. Early puppet animation was developed in eastern Europe where there is a long tradition of designing and carving puppets and dolls. These puppets were generally made of wood onto which features and clothing were painted. Occasionally the clothing was made of real cloth. The puppets were usually characters in animated folktales.

Today animated puppets are made from a variety of materials, including wood, metal, rubber, plastics, and clay. The puppet armature is of prime importance, as a weak skeletal structure will not support the weight of the figure. A common support is strong wire that holds the limbs of the puppet in position. The wire can hold the figure in place by attaching it to its base through holes beneath the feet of the puppet. The pieces of wire are removable so that the position of the puppet can be changed.

Whichever material the animator chooses for this type of animation, the figure must be solid, not only for support, but also for accurate movement. If the puppet is distorted during the course of manipulation, every unintentional movement will be detected onscreen.

The method of using clay as a material for stop motion animation is referred to as clay animation. Clay is a material that can be molded and modelled well, either with standard modelling clay or its plasticine substitute. Unlike some puppet animation techniques that may require a series of changeable facial masks to create mobile facial movement, clay can be easily manipulated in an animated progression.

Most of the work in stop motion occurs in the preproduction phase. All camera and figure positions are predetermined in relationship to the soundtrack. Special attention must be paid to the surface finish on all artwork, as the magnification of the work will tend to show any irregularities. The sets must be solid so they will not shift during production. Lighting and camera movements must be rehearsed prior to final shooting. It is important that great care be taken in the preproduction phase to avoid errors during the final shoot, as a mistake in the middle of a scene usually means that the sequence must be shot over again.

Another form of direct animation is the pinscreen that was developed in the 1930s by Alexander Alexieff and Claire Parker. Their film "Night on Bald Mountain" employs this technique. The pinscreen is a large white board through which many thousands of thin pins are inserted. By changing the lengths and depths of the pins in the board, variations in shading from black to white are created. These can be manipulated into shapes and forms that are gradually animated frame by frame. A tool is used to push each individual pin into its desired depth. The pinscreen image has a unique quality of soft-edged definition and image change. (See Figures 1.24, 1.25, 1.26, and 1.27.)

The camera setup for direct animation is determined by the method of working. A vertical animation stand overlooking the artwork from above is suitable for drawing, cutout animation, and manipulating paints, pastels, or any other flat material. In working with three dimensional objects, however, it may be preferable to mount the camera across from the subject so that the animation set can be designed on a horizontal plane. Depth of field (i.e., the range of acceptable focus) is not a problem in working with flat artwork. However, it becomes an important consideration in object animation since the objects are moving in three dimensions. The camera lens and position should accommodate the need for the desired depth of focus.

The lighting of three-dimensional objects is another creative element in direct animation and can be used to enhance and emphasize the intentions of the animation.

1.24

1.25

1.26

1.27

1.24 Pinscreen still from "Mindscape" by Jacques Drouin. Photo courtesy of National Film Board of Canada.

1.25 Pinscreen setup with image from "Mindscape" by Jacques Drouin. Photo courtesy of National Film Board of Canada.

1.26 Pinscreen setup with camera in left foreground. Image from "Mindscape" by Jacques Drouin. Photo courtesy of National Film Board of Canada.

1.27 Jacques Drouin working with the pinscreen. Photo courtesy of National Film Board of Canada.

1.28

Animation executed with cutouts can be very exciting. Using a simple cutout character allows the animator to concentrate on movement technique and timing, rather than on drawing. It is also an excellent opportunity to experiment with stylized motion. Cutout animation allows for a fresh approach to animating, but unless executed with finesse, it can have a rather unfinished appearance.

There are certain considerations that can help to avoid this result. The edges of the cutout shape should be cut finely with a razor blade unless they are to be intentionally coarse. The cutout can be attached to the background surface with a gentle adhesive, such as double stick tape or spray glue, to keep the object from moving around unintentionally while being filmed. If a character has parts that are drawn in multiple positions to give an animated effect (such as three facial positions moving from a frontal to a side view), the cutouts should be registered with some guidelines to insure precise movement. The cutout technique relies on the animator's ability to understand movement and is one that can improve with experience.

The cutout method can also be done with more preplanning and control than, for example, direct animation under the camera. By adhering cutout forms onto registered cels or paper, collage artwork can be created for each frame. Often, the combination of a more spontaneous approach with preplanned artwork results in the most interesting work.

Photographs can be used effectively in creating collage animation. Live-action film can be printed frame by frame as black and white photographic prints. They can then be artistically embellished with oil paints or altered with cel overlays. Sequences of photographs can be obtained as well, using a motorized 35 mm still camera that can shoot up to ten shots per

1.28 Collage animation sequence.

26

second. Such a photographic series can be handpainted, cut up, and mounted on registered cels. The images can then be incorporated into any desired background and rephotographed on the animation stand. Depending on the number of images per second, the animation may be more jerky than realistic movement. However, such a method has its own particular quality and feeling.

xerox animation

Xeroxing was originally used by animation studios to transfer the pencil drawings onto cels. The Xerox process was adopted as a way to free inkers from the tedious task of retracing animation drawings. The first results lacked subtlety. The transferred lines were a harsh, dark black color, and had a somewhat sketchy appearance. Any light lines from the original drawings would often drop out entirely. Now the Xerox process provides the animator with a wide range of colors to choose from, and the line quality has a softer, more graceful look.

Xeroxing has also been used as a way to reduce drawings in perspective. For example, to create animation of a character running away into the distance, the animator need only draw the scene once at any scale and Xerox it accordingly to reduce and/or enlarge it.

Color Xeroxing has been explored as an alternative to inking and painting for images that remain the same from frame to frame. For example, if a car is travelling across the frame, its basic form does not change even though it is moving. The color model for the car could be color Xeroxed for each frame of the move. Each copy of the car is then cut out and mounted onto cels to be laid over the background. Color Xeroxing produces a particular color quality and texture that differs from any other method of coloring and may be uniquely suitable for specific purposes.

1.29

1.29 Xerox animation sequence.

1.30

The potential to expeditiously create multiple copies of the same image sparked the imagination of some animators who saw it as a new working method. Using a Copyflo machine, live action film can be Xeroxed frame by frame onto a roll of paper. A fine grain black and white film stock is advisable for this technique, as the quality of the Xerox will be crisp and more easily read for details. Negative film stock can be used to create a reversed image, and the frame size can be controlled. The quality of the image is a unique one, and this technique offers many possibilities for creating artwork for animation.

matte box animation
A matte box, sometimes called a compendium, is a device made of a bellows that is attached to the front of the camera body and supported by rails. The back of the matte box holds a variety of gelatin filters and mattes of various shapes. A positive matte is a piece of black card stock that is cut out to obscure a specific area of the film frame. Its negative matte obscures the rest of the frame. (See Figure 1.30.)

When shooting with mattes, the film is exposed with the positive matte. It is then rewound and the negative matte is inserted in its place. A new scene is exposed onto the areas of the frame that had previously been left unexposed by the positive matte. In this way, for instance, half of the frame could be exposed with one scene of artwork and half with another scene. Using a matte box, however, is a very imprecise way of creating such an effect. Intricate shapes cannot be matted out this way, and a soft-edged matte line is always apparent. To achieve more refined matte work, an optical printer must be used. This will be discussed in the following section.

optical printing
Optical printing is the precise and controlled rephotography of one piece of film onto another. It is included as an animation tech-

1.30 Positive and negative mattes.

nique because it deals with creating each frame of film separately. An optical printer is essentially a projector facing a camera, with the camera lens focused on the film in the projector gate and illuminated by a lamp from the rear. The camera and projector gate have synchronous, motorized movements, so that motion picture frames can be copied from the camera "original" onto any frame of the "print" film. An optical printer is used to create simple effects, such as freezing the image, fading in and out of the picture, cross-dissolving from one scene to another, superimposing one sequence over another, reversing action, skipping frames to quicken the pacing, eliminating unwanted sections of the film, and step-printing to slow the motion down. By inserting colored gels between the camera and projector, you can get the optical printer to add color to already existing footage. You can create precise multiple split screens by exposing different areas of the film frame with different images, while using positive and negative mattes between the camera and projector.

You can use an optical printer to combine multiple film elements onto a single piece of film. Suppose you want to have a live action woman walking across the sky. You rotoscope film of the woman walking in order to create male and female mattes for her form. The male matte has the dark portion in the center and is clear on the outside. The female matte is clear in the middle and dark on the outside. These mattes are made by either cutting her form out of black flint paper and mounting each matte onto a cel, or painting her form in black onto cels. These mattes are shot on high-contrast film, and a male and female version are printed. The positive or male matte of the woman is bipacked into the projector directly on top of the camera original of the sky. This is filmed. The black shape of the woman is seen by the camera as an unexposed area, and the surrounding sky is now exposed. The camera is rewound with a closed or capped shutter, and the camera original of the woman is bipacked with the female matte and filmed. The black area is then exposed to the woman walking, and the sky area blocked out. In the resulting film, the woman is, indeed, walking in the sky. (See Figure 1.31.)

Bipacking can also be done directly in camera. This technique requires an animation camera that accepts a bipack magazine that allows the loading of two pieces of film at a time. In this case, the raw stock and positive matte element are threaded together in the camera. When the artwork is shot, the area that is covered by the matte will remain unexposed. The film is then rewound, the negative matte loaded with the raw stock, and new artwork exposed onto the unexposed areas of the film.

The choice of bipacking or optical printing of multiple elements is partially a matter of the preference of the cameraman. Generally, for more complex combinations, the optical printer is selected because it is more precise, and registration of all the elements is essential.

To insure proper alignment with the optical printer, targets need to be made. These are pieces of film containing details with coinciding information, placed in the printer gate and the camera gate and adjusted to a one-to-one correspondence. This is realized by looking through the camera prism focused on the film plane. If this relationship is not formed, the resulting work will have a wobbly appearance, due to its being out of alignment.

The optical printer provides accurate color control by the combination of different colored gels at specific and different exposures. There are six colors available in varying densities ranging from .025 to .50 mm used as color correction filters. Three are primary colors—green, red, and blue, and three are secondary colors—magenta, cyan, and yellow, which correspondingly act as opposites to the primary colors. If you want to subtract green from an image, a magenta gel should be used. If magenta were to be subtracted, then a green gel would be used. All colors must be tested before the final optical is shot to determine the exact exposures for proper color reproduction.

The extent of elements that can be combined and effects that can be created on the optical printer are enormous. With the computerized control of optical benches, the potential of optical effects continues to improve and increase.

1.31 Traveling mattes used to composite separate film elements. Cloud background is exposed with black matte of woman. Woman is matted onto cloud background by using clear matte and original film of woman.

computer animation

From micro to mainframe, the computer is being used more and more extensively in the field of animation. Video games in the home and the arcade are full of animated graphics. Commercially available programs for the home computer allow for the creation of fairly sophisticated, albeit low-resolution, animation. The larger, more powerful mainframe computers have been programmed to create stunning animation and graphics for feature films and commercial use. Depending on the particular hardware and software involved, the computer serves several different kinds of functions.

Motion control is the use of a computer to automate the operation of an animation stand. Because of its precision, the computer-operated animation stand enables the creation of special effects and graphics that could not be achieved otherwise. To create, for example, the effect of an animated, translucent, streaking trail of light that bends and twists and follows the path of a car traveling along a road requires the addition of computer assistance to control the precision of the camera. The computer-operated camera can retrace its own complex movements to a much more accurate degree than a manually operated camera. This feature is essential in creating sophisticated special graphic effects.

An analogue computer system enables the manipulation of existing artwork on videotape. The image is scanned into the computer with a video camera. Then, in real time, the image can be stretched, flipped, distorted, and colorized by the manipulation of programmable operations until the desired result is reached.

The analogue signal is understood by the computer to be continuous data, whereas the digital signal is made up of discreet units of data. A digital computer can generate its own graphics and animate them as well. Each computer may be programmed differently, and thus each computer's graphic abilities are slightly different. Sometimes a computer will generate forms based on information that is typed into it on its keyboard. For example, a line may be indicated by typing in the coordinates of its two end-

points. It is possible to "draw" an image into the computer using a special electronic light pen, or stylus, on a digitizing tablet. Every point that the stylus touches on the tablet is registered in the computer and displayed on its monitor in the equivalent position. There are also light pens that allow the artist to draw directly on the television screen. And graphic information can be entered into the computer using a "mouse," a small, enclosed device that fits into the palm of a hand and is pushed around on any surface to indicate the image to be drawn.

Computer imagery can be displayed as either vector or raster graphics, depending on the nature of the hardware and software in use. A vector display presents forms as a series of smooth lines drawn on the screen from point to point. A raster display, on the other hand, breaks the image into individual points that are combined to create a given graphic.

The simplest digital imagery is a two-dimensional linear form. Some digital computers produce three dimensional vector graphics, based on the information that describes a given form, and display these images in a skeletal "wire-frame" format. If the computer is programmed to create only black and white artwork, color can be added in an optical printer after the film has been generated by the computer. More sophisticated programs allow for fully colored, shaded, and textured three-dimensional forms.

The computer can be programmed to understand space, dimension, and perspective. It can rotate images of objects and revolve around them. It can reproduce forms and move them from one given point to another. It can change their colors. It can make them appear to zoom away from us, or zoom toward us and right past our view. Some computers are programmed to produce a variety of high resolution textures which can be "mapped" onto any three-dimensional image to become its new surface.

Computers have been programmed to create "in-betweens" to assist the animation process. The computer is able to create the requested number of drawings to metamorphose from one key drawing to the next. Because the computer program calculates by using mathematical equations, any pauses, rhythms, or added gestures have to be specially written into the in-betweening program.

The computer can also be useful in the coloring stage of the animation procedure. If all the drawings for an animated film have been made in the computer, then adding color to them is simply a matter of indicating which color is to be added to which areas of the image by touching down on the area with the light pen. The computer fills up the indicated area very quickly and neatly and can proceed to the next color immediately without waiting for any paint to dry.

Live-action footage can be digitized by a video scan that assigns a numerical value indicating color or gray tone to every point of every frame. The image is essentially translated into information stored in the computer's memory. When digitized live action is combined with computer-generated imagery, the two blend indistinguishably, suggesting infinite possibilities for special film effects.

One of the few computer animation systems that is affordable and practical for the individual user is MOVIE MAKER , designed by Interactive Picture Systems, Inc. MOVIE MAKER is a versatile, easy-to-use animation system that operates in a microcomputer environment and provides for the creation of real-time animation and soundtrack, albeit low resolution. No programming knowledge is required to use MOVIE MAKER, as it often is with higher resolution, mainframe computer animation systems. The hardware can cost as little as $1000, and the MOVIE MAKER software costs $150.

MOVIE MAKER is designed to emulate traditional cel animation. The process is divided into four stages. COMPOSE is the step in which you draw and paint the equivalent of the animation cels. Backgrounds are created as separate elements.

The next step is to RECORD these sequences onto the background. Recording can be done either in real time or single frame, and characters are recorded one by one, building up to six "actors" on the screen at once.

Sound is recorded during this phase of MOVIE MAKER. Like the recording of the sequences, sound effects are built one track at a time, up to four tracks. The system provides numerous pre-existing sounds and musical notes. RECORD also provides the ability to record color and zoom changes, to erase a given frame or series of frames, to reposition a specific character, or to delete it entirely.

The third phase is SMOOTH, the equivalent of the film laboratory, during which all of the computer data for the animation, background, and sound is compiled.

The fourth stage is PLAY, comparable to projecting a finished film. The animation plays back in its final form.

Although MOVIE MAKER runs on a personal computer and lacks the resolution and memory capabilities of mainframe animation systems, it is truly a powerful tool for animators, designers, and home users. Unlike the mainframe systems, MOVIE MAKER is readily available and accessible to most everyone.

Advancements in the field of computer graphics and animation are being made very rapidly and continuously as computer programmers and film designers learn to understand and communicate with each other. The potential to create new kinds of imagery is constantly expanding.

The following section of color plates is a selection of frames of computer animation created by using a range of hardware and software technologies, and produced by the most sophisticated computer graphics production companies, frequently for advertising and commercial purposes.

camera activity
The relationship of the camera to the artwork for each frame of animation is an important element in the design of the animation. The

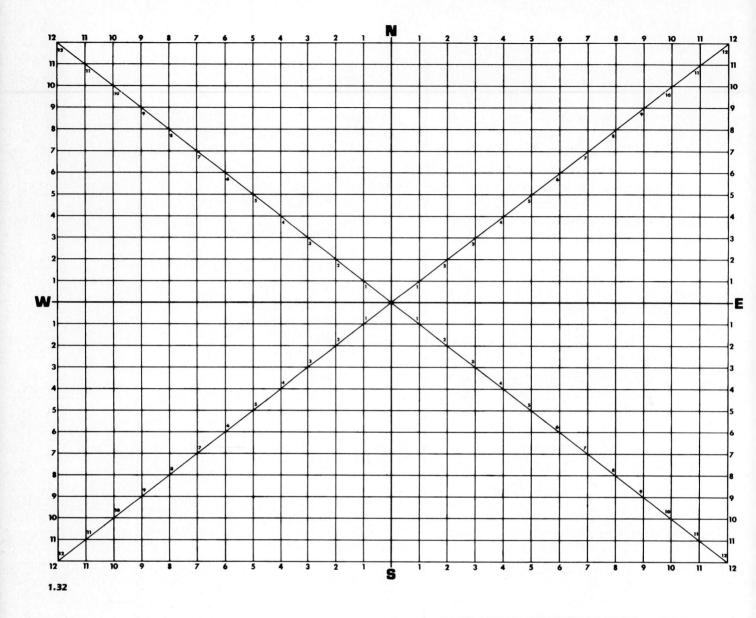

1.32

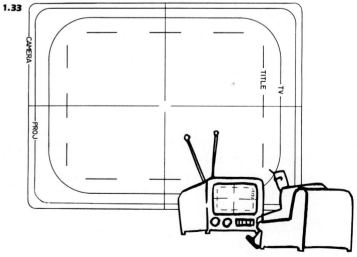

1.33

1.32 16 mm animation field guide indicating twelve field sizes for artwork.

1.33 Standard framing guide. The outer rectangle indicates what area the camera aperture frames. The next rectangle inside that indicates what framing will be projected. The rounded rectangle inside that indicates TV cutoff. The dotted rectangle indicates the safe title area.

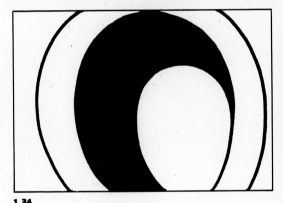

1.34

camera can zoom up and down, and the animation table that holds the artwork can move north, south, east, and west, and rotate in a full circle in minute and controlled increments. The placement of the camera in every frame is another variable that the animator must consider in creating animation artwork.

In planning artwork, the size and framing of the field must be selected in the proper proportions. Later, when the artwork is being shot, the camera must frame the same field in which the artwork was drawn. The dimensions of the rectangular area framed by the camera lens have a standard aspect ratio of 1.376 to 1, or 4 to 3, width to height, unless a special wide screen lens with a different aspect ratio is used. A field guide is the standard reference for the proper framing ratios of the artwork so that they will match exactly the camera's aspect ratio. It is a thick, flexible, clear chart made up of concentric rectangles that the animator and cameraperson use for layouts. It shows all the various sizes at which a piece of artwork can be filmed in relation to the motion picture film frame. The lens of the camera is closer to the artwork at different field sizes and farther away at the larger sizes. It is important to note that a television monitor cuts off part of the film frame when it displays the image. If possible, design artwork in relation to what the final display medium will be. (See Figure 1.32 and 1.33.)

Artwork can be made on a very large field or a very small field. Its size on the film will be determined by how the camera is positioned to frame that artwork. The camera can be moved closer to or further away from the artwork frame by frame to create zooms. (Figure 1.34.) The artwork itself can be moved frame by frame below the camera to produce horizontal, vertical, and diagonal panning movements. (Figure 1.35.) The animation table can be moved 360° or more frame by frame to create a spinning movement on the film. The combination of any of these

1.34 Three-frame zooming sequence of the word "zoom."

34 moves, although time-consuming, can greatly enhance and energize the choreography of a sequence of animation.

The speed and smoothness of these moves are determined by the ratio of the size of the artwork to the field size in relation to the increments of change for each frame. In order to avoid an abrupt start and stop, it is useful to ease in and out, or accelerate and decelerate, with such moves. This means that the beginning increments of change start out very small and gradually build up to the move's constant rate of change. At the end of the move, the increments decrease gradually in order to smooth out the move's stop.

The animation camera can create fade-ins, fade-outs, and dissolves from one image to the next (Figure 1.36). Superimpositions can be made by shooting one scene, rewinding the film with the shutter closed, or capped, and exposing the film with a new scene or multiple scenes. These techniques can be used at the discretion of the animator for various effects.

The ability of the camera to rewind film and reexpose it over and over again with new imagery allows for the creation of multiple pass backlit motion graphics. This is a technique of combining several backlit art elements onto one piece of film by multiple shooting runs. The artwork can be made of high-contrast Kodalith film and combinations of colored gels. Only one area of the frame is exposed per run. Thus, each color can be controlled individually, and quality remains at a maximum. In addition, because the backlight is passing directly through the colored gel and into the camera lens to expose the film, colors in backlit animation tend to be more intense and vibrant than in toplit artwork. Backlit animation is often used to produce a more graphically stylized look than cel or drawn animation can provide.

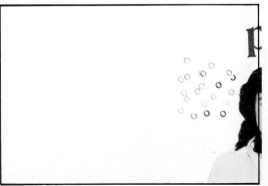

1.35 Left to right pan.

1.36

As with the optical printer, the animation camera can be used to do bipacking and traveling mattes by running two pieces of film through the camera at once. An example of the use of the animation stand to do this is for the matting of an animated character into a live-action scene. Hand-painted or cutout black mattes must be made for each frame of the animated character. The live-action footage is loaded into the camera with the raw stock, and the mattes are exposed onto the film. The film is then rewound, and the animated character that conforms to the matte is shot against black. Its image is exposed into the previously matted out areas of the film, and thereby combined with the live action.

The aerial image animation stand is specially designed for the combination of live-action and toplit animation with only one pass of the film through the camera. The live action scene is rear-projected and focused by a pair of condenser lenses onto the plane of the cutout area of the animation table where the toplit artwork is laid. The design works so that the top lighting does not obliterate the rear-projected image. It is important that the toplit artwork be opaque enough to prevent the rear-projected image from exposing through it. The live scene is advanced one frame at a time, and the next piece of artwork is changed correspondingly, and thus, frame by frame, the two scenes are combined. (See Figure 1.37.)

As previously mentioned, a computer can be used to assist camera activity, thereby creating certain effects that could not otherwise have been produced. This technology is known as <u>motion control</u>. The computer is programmed to control the movements of the camera and animation stand frame by frame. It can move the table, move the camera, and expose a single frame of film, according to programmed instructions. Motion control facilitates complex camera

1.36 Fade out to black.

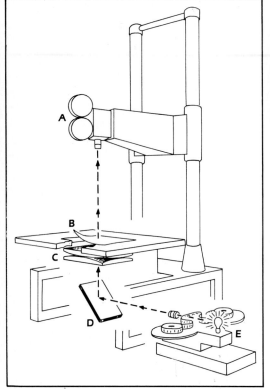

1.37

A. Camera

B. Animation or title on clear cel

C. Condenser lenses

D. 45° mirror

E. Motion picture projector synchronized with camera.

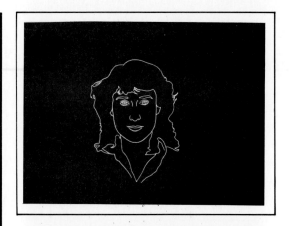

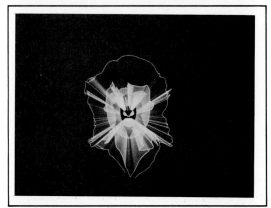

1.38

1.37 Aerial image animation stand.

1.38 Two variations of a streak made from black and white line artwork.

moves, making them much faster and free from any human error. Computer control of the shooting allows for precise repetition of camera moves, enabling complex multipass work to remain accurately registered and two or more complex moves to match each other perfectly.

Computer-assisted shooting has produced a refinement of the "streak" in motion graphics. A streak is a trail of translucent light that is left by an object or a word. It is created by zooming on a piece of backlit artwork with the shutter open on one frame for the full length of the zoom. In other words, each frame of a zoom is shot as the full zoom itself with the shutter open on each frame. The result is a light trail on each frame, which is seen as an animated streak when the film is projected. The streak is an effect that is commonly used in commercial graphics and special effects. A simple streak can be created without the assistance of a computer, but it is a time-consuming and demanding task. Because of the numerous repetitions of the same move, the computer enables the production of more dramatic and intricate streaking activity. (See Figure 1.38.)

Slit scan is a special effects technique that is possible only with a computer-assisted animation stand. Basically, it is a photographic method of stretching or elongating an image that is normally flat. The artwork is shot through a slit or a series of slits onto one frame of film at a time. The film is held in the camera gate, in front of the lens aperture, with the shutter open as the camera moves in complex paths. The film is then advanced one frame, the shutter held open again, and the camera move repeated exactly. The resulting effects are that a dot becomes a line, a line becomes a two-dimensional figure, and a two-dimensional figure becomes three-dimensional. If the artwork is moved as well, walls of light and color are created, as if the camera were traveling through a tunnel. A classic example of the slit scan method can be seen in the "stargate" segment in 2001: A Space Odyssey. Slit scan is one step beyond streaking. Instead of trails of light being formed, shapes and colors of light patterns are created dependent on the movement of the camera and artwork and the number and shapes of the slits beneath the camera.

Thus the camera activity in its relation to the artwork must be considered carefully by the animation designer. To communicate his or her intentions clearly to the cameraperson, the designer uses exposure sheets. Exposure sheets are standard instruction forms that account for every change in artwork and camera position in each frame. They indicate what the combination of cel layers should be and what the field size should be, as well as any fades, dissolves, or superimpositions. Every frame must be accounted for. Exposure sheets are an invaluable guide for the cameraperson so that the animation will be shot to obtain the intended results. (See Figure 2.12 in the section entitled "Shooting The Animation.")

the
film
production

112

After the graphic styles and techniques have been determined, a number of further stages must be addressed before the animation can be considered to be a finished film. This chapter discusses these stages of the film production and the decisions that must be made as the production evolves.

the format

Film is available in different sizes, referred to as "format." The format of the film indicates the width and frame size of the stock and is measured in millimeters. The choice of format determines the kind of equipment used in making the film, its budget, and its eventual use (see Figure 2.2).

Super-8 film is the smallest, least expensive of film stocks. It is an updated version of 8 mm film, but with a slightly larger frame size. Super-8 equipment is light and portable, and a camera and projector can be purchased fairly inexpensively. Super-8 sound equipment is available, either as single system or double system. In single system, the sound is recorded onto a magnetic strip that is part of the film stock. It is convenient for shooting with synchronized, or "sync," sound, but it is difficult to edit sound and picture if the sound is to be created as a separate element. Double system entails a separate Super-8, with a sprocketed, magnetic sound track that can be edited to the image more conveniently.

Super-8 film can be used for rotoscoping artwork that can later be shot onto 16 mm film. It

can also serve as an inexpensive "sketch" medium for experimentation and testing.

The projection quality of Super-8 film is not as good as 16 mm or 35 mm because the small frame size loses resolution when it is blown up on a big screen. This is an important consideration in the choice of format.

Super-8 film is a good medium for home movies, but professionally, it is not widely used. Projection facilities are not readily available, and labs and optical houses are generally not equipped to work in Super-8. Super-8 can be transferred fairly well to videotape, which is a widely accepted viewing medium. In summary, although Super-8 is a convenient and affordable way of working, it has serious limitations that must be weighed when selecting a format.

Independent filmmakers commonly use 16 mm film. It holds up well in projection and transfer to videotape, and screening facilities for 16 mm are commonly available in many theaters and professional studios. There is a large selection of film stocks in color and black and white to suit a wide range of purposes and needs.

For use with 16 mm film, the Bolex is a reasonably priced camera with the ability to shoot single frames for animation. Good quality lenses can be purchased for the Bolex, and it can be fitted onto a variety of animation stands.

The 35 mm format remains the commercially accepted standard for animation in both feature films and advertising. Because its frame size

2.1

is larger, the image quality is excellent. In shooting animation artwork that may be meticulously detailed and carefully rendered, it is important that the reproduction quality be as high as possible. Although 35 mm stock and lab costs are higher than 16 mm or Super-8, it is often well worth the cost to shoot animation on 35 mm, especially since, in animation, film and lab costs are generally not the major part of the production budget.

The Oxberry animation stand is probably the highest quality stand made, and its cameras are adaptable to either 16 mm or 35 mm film. The Oxberry's features include a motorized zoom with automatic focusing; an automatic fade and dissolve mechanism; north, south, east, west, diagonal, and circular table movements; and top and bottom registration pegbars that can be cranked left and right independently of each other. All these features are numerically calibrated, so all movements of the camera and table can be calculated and controlled in very small increments. The Oxberry also permits the addition of a computer to assist in its shooting. It is an extremely expensive piece of equipment, but its high level of mechanical precision and dependability make it an excellent shooting tool for animation.

It is possible to make blowups and reductions from one format to another. Film shot originally as Super-8 can be reprinted optically as 16 mm or 35 mm, and conversely, 35 mm can be printed as 16 mm film. This becomes necessary when combining footage of different formats into a single film. It is also useful in making prints of the same film for different projection formats. Remember, however, that this process takes the film one generation away from its original.

The choice of format depends on the intended use of the final film. For small personal works,

2.2

2.2 Film formats (enlarged).
Left to right: Super-8, 16 mm, 35 mm.

Super-8 may be the best choice. If you intend to screen the film theatrically and distribute it, 16 mm is a suitable selection. In professional and commercial animation work, 35 mm film is the standard format.

film stocks

There is a variety of film stocks available in 16 mm and 35 mm. The choice of stock depends on the desired look of the final film. Film comes in black and white or color, and as reversal or negative. When reversal stock is shot and processed, it results in a positive image—that is, an image where the dark areas of the artwork are dark and the light areas are light on the film. Reversal color film reproduces the colors of the artwork. Negative film stock, on the other hand, produces a negative image of the artwork. A print from the negative is made to obtain a positive image. Both reversal and negative stock are available in color and black and white.

High contrast film stock produces an image that translates tones into either black or white, and minimizes gray tones. It can be processed as either negative or positive, and is used to create positive and negative mattes for optical printing and bipacking. (Refer to pages 27–29.)

Each film stock has a different sensitivity to light. This characteristic is known as the speed of the film and is indicated by a number referred to as ASA in the United States and DIN in Europe. The higher the number, the faster the film and the more sensitive it is to light. Conversely, a low ASA indicates a film stock that is slower and requires more light for proper exposure. Faster film stocks result in grainier image reproduction; slower film produces a finer grain. In shooting animation, generally the amount of light can be easily controlled, and the problem of inadequate light does not arise. Thus, the choice of film stock is not restricted by the speed of the film.

Different stocks are more or less sensitive to different ranges of the color spectrum. Daylight film, which is used outdoors, is less sensitive to blue tones. Tungsten film, which is used with artificial light sources, is less sensitive to reds and oranges. For animation that is shot on a stand and lit with artificial light, tungsten film should be selected for proper color reproduction. Kodak (Eastman Kodak Company, Technical Publications Department, Rochester, New York 14608) publishes guides that describe the characteristics of all its film stocks. It is useful to test various stocks in order to actually see how an image will be reproduced by each one and to determine the most desirable film stock for a particular project. It is important to remember that if different film stocks are used in various shootings and cut together as one final film, the quality of the image will vary slightly. To avoid this, the same film stock should be used throughout the project to provide a constant quality of reproduction. Additionally, if a scene of animation is to be cut into a longer film, it must be shot on matching stock. If the longer film stock is negative, the animation must also be shot on negative.

the camera

This section provides a basic explanation of the mechanical workings of a motion picture camera, which may be helpful in understanding the film production process from animation artwork to finished film.

The camera, as well as the projector, makes use of the principle of intermittent motion. Intermittent motion allows film to move through the camera at a constant rate and at the same time allows each frame to be retained in the gate for a fraction of a second.

The gate is the path in front of the lens through which the film travels. The aperture is the rectangular opening in the gate through which light passes to expose the film frame that is in front of it. A pressure plate holds the film firmly against the gate so it travels smoothly. There are small movable metal claws in the gate area that engage the sprocket holes of the film and pull it through the gate frame by frame. Two loops in the threading of the film through the camera create the proper tension to enable one frame to be held briefly in the gate while the film con-

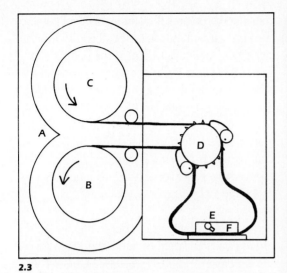

tinues a constant motion through the camera. The <u>shutter</u> is a semicircular metal disk that rotates once per frame of film. As the open area of the shutter passes in front of the aperture, light is permitted to enter and expose the frame of film that is being held in front of the gate. The shutter rotates 24 times a second when continuous action is being filmed. Thus each frame is actually being exposed to light for approximately 1/48 second in live action. The actual shutter speed varies from camera to camera. In an animation camera, the shutter is designed to rotate more slowly. In an Oxberry, for instance, singe-frame shutter speed is 1/6 second per rotation.

To expose one frame of film, the claws engage the sprocket holes, pull a frame into position in front of the gate, and hold it there as the shutter rotates once, letting in light. As the shutter rotates to its closed position, the claws pull the next frame into position, and the exposure continues.

Some cameras, including an Oxberry, are equipped with a second independent shutter, known as a <u>variable shutter</u>. It is regulated separately and can be closed down or opened up gradually to create fades and dissolves.

A good animation camera, then, has specific requirements. Most important, it must be able to shoot one frame at a time. It should have a very accurate registration system to hold the film securely in the gate as each frame is being exposed. This is accomplished by an additional set of registration pins that engage a second set of sprocket holes in the film. An animation camera should have the ability to go backward to allow for dissolving and superimposition. It should, as well, have a reflex viewing system so that it is easy to see what the lens sees for framing and focusing of artwork. A <u>reflex view-</u>

2.3 Simplified threading diagram of the inside of a camera, showing (A) magazine that holds the film stock; (B) unexposed film; (C) exposed film; (D) sprocket wheel; (E) shuttle; (F) pressure plate.

44

ing system is a camera feature that, by means of mirrors, enables the cameraman to see directly through the lens. In nonreflex cameras, a separate viewing system, or viewfinder, must be used to determined what the lens is framing. However, viewfinder systems present the problem of parallax—that is, the slight difference between what the lens sees and what the viewfinder sees. When using a nonreflex camera, you must account for parallax before establishing the final image framing.

There are several ways in which the film is advanced through the camera. The most basic is a spring wind, often found in the Bolex camera. As the spring unwinds, the shutter may lose some of its speed, causing minor fluctuations in the exposure time and resulting in uneven exposures of individual frames. This problem is solved by using an electrically driven motorized camera. The Oxberry is controlled by a motor, and thus the shutter speed and exposure time remain constant.

The lens fits onto the camera in front of the aperture. It focuses the image of the artwork onto the film plane. The focal length of the lens, measured in millimeters, determines its angle of view. A wide-angle lens sees a broader image. A telephoto lens magnifies the image for a closer view, which is important in determining the framing of the artwork. A zoom lens offers a range of focal lengths in one lens. Although this provides flexibility in the framing of an image, the quality of the image tends to be better when using prime lenses rather than a zoom lens.

The focal length also effects depth of field—that is, the range of acceptable focus that the lens sees. In filming flat artwork, this is not a major concern, since there is only one plane of depth. It does become important in the filming of three-dimensional objects, however.

The focal length that most closely approximates "normal" (that is, what the human eye sees) is a 25 mm lens in 16 mm cameras and a 50 mm lens in 35 mm cameras.

An adjustable iris at the back of the lens near the film plane regulates the amount of light coming into the camera. It is adjusted according to the light meter reading to obtain the correct exposure of the film. The iris setting determines the size of the aperture and is called the F stop. F-stops are calibrated on the lens from 1.0 to 1.4, 2, 2.8, 4, 5.6, 8, 11, 16, and 22. Each successive F-stop cuts the light by exactly half. F/5.6 allows half as much light to expose the film as F/4. Conversely, F/4 allows twice as much light as F/5.6, and eight times as much light as F/11.

The F-stop also affects the depth of field. When there is a great deal of light, the iris must be closed down and the F-stop will be higher. The higher the F-stop, the larger the depth of field. Conversely, when there is less light, the iris is opened up and the depth of field is more limited.

Several attachments are available for motion picture cameras that facilitate single-frame shooting for animation. When the exposure of a frame is not electronic, a cable release can be attached to the shutter release. A cable release is a flexible metal rod that triggers the shutter release from a distance of several feet, replacing the need to push the trigger by hand. This helps to avoid the possibility of inadvertently jerking or moving the camera when a frame is being exposed (see Figure 2.4).

An intervalometer is an auxiliary variable-speed motor that can be attached to the camera to regulate the intervals at which each frame is exposed. It can be set, for example, to shoot a frame every 15 seconds or every 15 minutes, and it is used in time-lapse cinematography when the camera is left for long periods of time single-framing an event.

A matte box is a device rigged onto the camera; it sits between the lens and the artwork. It is used to hold filters or mattes to create in-camera effects such as split screens and animated wipes across the frame to make a transition from one scene to another. The matte box is used to produce the familiar "keyhole" view. One inserts a cutout keyhole shape into the matte box in front of the artwork while shooting.

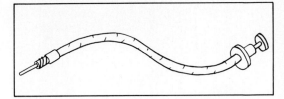
2.4

2.5

The animation stand is an assembly used to hold the camera while the artwork is being shot frame by frame. It determines the relationship between the camera and the subject, an important consideration in the design of a film. Most commonly, in shooting flat artwork, the camera is mounted above the table top aiming down. For shooting three-dimensional animation, the camera may be mounted to shoot the subject horizontally, or at any preferred angle. Depending on the nature of the artwork and the style of the film, a smooth interaction between the camera and the subject may be desirable.

The animation stand may provide camera movement—up, down, and, at times, at various angles. It may also provide for the movement of the artwork in north, south, east, west, diagonal, and circular directions.

The most basic method of mounting a camera is on a tripod sturdy enough to hold it securely. A fluid head tripod allows for panning and tilting movements, as well as zooming up and down. A tripod is an inexpensive and portable way to create a workable animation setup.

The camera can also be mounted on a copy stand. However, because of the design of the copy stand, the camera mount requires that the artwork be shot upside down, which, depending on the nature of the artwork, may or may not be a disadvantage.

An alternative is to construct a homemade animation stand to accommodate personal needs and styles of working. With a little ingenuity, plywood and two-by-fours can be used, or bathroom pipes may serve the purpose. A stand

2.4 The cable release is attached to the shutter release mechanism on the camera. The plunger on the end pushes the metal rod and activates the shutter release to expose a frame of film. On a spring-wound camera, the cable release enables single-frame shooting without physical contact that could accidentally move the camera.

2.5 A zoom is created as the camera is moved closer and closer to the artwork.

can be designed using a tripod head to hold the camera and a second tripod head to hold the table top, so that the relationship between the camera and the subject can be in variable and controllable flux.

Depending on individual requirements, an animation stand can be designed to incorporate easy up-and-down zoom movement of the camera, as well as easy table-top movement of the artwork for panning. A calibration system is useful for determining and calculating the exact positions and movements of both camera and artwork. The animation stand should provide a convenient registration system for shooting the artwork that corresponds to that on which the artwork has been created. A movable piece of glass can be installed to serve as a platen to hold multiple layers of cel artwork flat and in place. If backlighting is desired, there should be a hole covered by translucent glass in the tabletop directly under the lens.

Professional animation stands incorporate all these elements, designed with mechanical precision and accuracy of plus or minus 1/100 inch. As previously mentioned, the most common professional stands for both 16 mm and 35 mm shooting are manufactured by Oxberry (Division of Richmark Camera Service, 180 Broad Street, Carlstadt, New Jersey 07072). Framing of artwork, movement of the tabletop, and camera zooms can be repeated exactly for reshoots and multiple camera passes over changing artwork. This ability may be enhanced by the addition of computerized camera operation. The camera zoom is motorized, and automatically adjusts its focus as it moves up and down. Fades and dissolves are also motorized and internally calibrated to be smooth at any selected frame rate from eight to 120 frames per second (see Figure 2.6).

2.6

2.6 Oxberry animation stand (center) with computer control (left) and console panel (right).
Table control dials for north, south, east, west, and circular motion are seen at the front of the stand.
Camera is mounted on the two vertical posts, focusing down at the table top. Zooms are created by sliding the camera up and down these posts.
A Pantograph is visible behind the console panel.

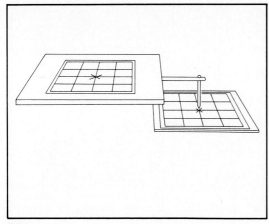

2.7

The viewfinder in the Oxberry camera provides a field guide that becomes visible over the artwork to assist in correct framing. It indicates the size of the film frame; the projected image, which is a little smaller; the television frame, which is further cropped; and the center of the frame.

The camera is also equipped with a pin registration system in the gate to ensure that the film frame is held securely in position when it is being exposed.

The Oxberry stand has its own peg registration system previously discussed. There are two pegbars on the stand, to hold both top-pegged and bottom-pegged artwork separately. A corresponding pegbar is available for making the artwork.

The platen on the Oxberry is a detachable, hinged piece of glass. The glass is optically corrected to minimize any distortion of the artwork. It can be easily raised and lowered. When it is raised, it clicks into a held position to facilitate the changing of artwork frame by frame. It is possible to attach the platen mechanism to a foot pedal, which raises and lowers it, so the cameraman has both hands free to change the artwork. When multiple layers of cels have to be changed for each new frame, the foot pedal becomes a welcome tool.

Several additional attachments increase the versatility of the Oxberry. One such device is the Pantograph, which facilitates the execution of complex camera movements over one image. The Pantograph is a specially designed platform with a movable pointer located to the side of the animation compound. The movement over the artwork is charted as a line on a separate piece of paper, which is placed onto the Pantograph platform. This line is marked with the points at

2.7 Pantograph. The pointer on the right follows a designated line of action, frame by frame. It in turn moves the table top on the left so that it is positioned below the camera to create the desired animated action. The Pantograph facilitates intricate camera moves on tabletop artwork.

which each frame will be shot. The pointer is connected to the tracking mechanism of the tabletop and aligned with the camera's field of view. As the cameraman moves the tabletop so that the pointer follows the direction line on the Pantograph, the camera traces the corresponding move over the artwork frame by frame. Such camera moves are possible without a Pantograph, but the Pantograph makes it easier to preplan and follow exactly any given move (see Figure 2.7 on page 47).

A <u>Gimbal Box</u> is a device rigged in the cutout area of the compound to allow for stop motion animation of small objects. It holds and manipulates the movement of an object frame by frame. The object must be small enough to fit into the cutout area and to remain within the depth of field of the lens. The combination of the Gimbal movement of the object, the compound movement, and the camera movement can provide great flexibility of animation to create such effects as flying around three-dimensional turning objects. Often, such animation is combined with other scenes of animation, such as backgrounds or special effects shot on separate passes of the film through the camera.

lighting

The lighting of the subject to be shot is another element that can be varied to obtain different effects in the final film.

For flat animation artwork, it is important that the light fall evenly across the subject area. Generally, two lights are used on either side of the artwork, hitting the artwork at an angle to avoid reflections into the camera lens (see Figure 2.8).

The lighting of a three-dimensional subject can be designed to produce the desired amount of shadow and contrast when the object is animated. Because animation shooting often takes

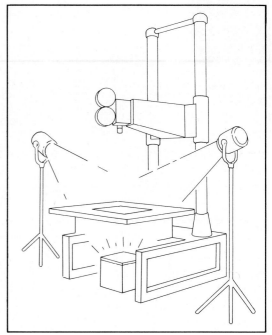

2.8

2.8 Lighting for animation. Top lighting is produced by two side lights aimed at artwork at a 45° angle. Bottom lighting is provided by light source below the cutout transluscent table top.

a long time, very hot light sources should be avoided. Lower intensity lights can be used, or the light sources can be set at a distance from the camera and artwork, to maintain a more comfortable temperature for the duration of the shoot.

The subject may be lit by a variety of sources. If the subject is to be shot outdoors, daylight may be sufficient. Indoor shooting can be lit with conventional household lightbulbs. Photofloods mounted in aluminum reflector scoops can be used. However, lightbulbs and photofloods slowly lose their intensity as they continue to burn. This can cause a noticeable change in exposure over the course of the shooting. Quartz bulbs are a good light source for animation. Although they are more expensive, their intensity remains constant throughout their lifetime, so exposure variation is not a problem.

Different light sources produce light of different temperatures and color ranges. Pure white light contains all the colors of the light spectrum. The exact color of a light depends on the temperature of its source. The human eye compensates for these subtle color differences, but film does not. Daylight is a hot light source, and contains more blue light than an artificial light source, which emits more red and orange light. The temperature of a light source is measured by the Kelvin Color Temperature Scale. A 60-watt lightbulb is 2800° K; quartz lights are 3200° K; noontime sunlight is 5400° K.

As previously discussed, film stock is manufactured with different chemical balances, which have different sensitivities to the light that hits them. In order to obtain color reproduction, the proper film stock must be selected depending on the temperature of the light source. Daylight-balanced film (5500° K) should be used for outdoor shooting. There are two types of tungsten film, one balanced for 3200° K and one for 3400° K. These should be used with artificial light sources, depending on the type of bulb being used. Artificial lights are generally available in either 3200° K or 3400° K. Fluorescent light is an unsatisfactory light source for faithful color reproduction because it is made up of an incomplete color spectrum. Unless the proper combination of filters has been determined, fluorescent light should be avoided in lighting the subject.

Lights can be rigged onto the sides of the animation stand and positioned permanently, or they can be mounted on movable light stands and repositioned for each different shoot. If the light source is fixed, the proper exposure can be established for various film stocks by one initial series of tests. If the light source is movable, the exposure setting must be adjusted for each new lighting setup.

light metering

A light meter measures the amount of light illuminating the subject. It is used to calculate the proper F-stop setting for the lens aperture to regulate the amount of light that enters the lens and exposes the film.

There are two types of light meters: incident and reflective. An incident meter measures the amount of light that falls onto the subject. For flat animation artwork, where the light falls evenly over the artwork, an incident light meter is suitable for measuring the light and determining the proper exposure. To obtain an incident reading, the meter is held close to the subject, facing the camera lens. In this way, the meter reacts to the same light that is hitting the subject. The meter should be moved over the area covered by the subject to ensure that lighting is even. A reflective light meter measures the amount of light reflected off the subject. A reflective reading is taken by holding the meter near the camera lens and aimed at the subject. For three-dimensional setups, the reflective meter can be used to measure the different amounts of light reflected by different areas of the subject. These differences should be evaluated and the F-stop set so that the light and dark areas of the subject will be exposed accordingly.

sound

The relationship between the sound and the image in a film is extremely important. In animation, just as the image can be controlled in every frame, the soundtrack as well can be compiled and synchronized to the image frame by frame, according to the desires of the filmmaker.

Sound can be made up of voices, music, and sound effects, combined and interwoven to communicate and strengthen the idea of the film. It can be created before the animation is done and used as a guide to the rhythm and timing of the picture. Or the film may be postscored—that is, the soundtrack is made after the film is shot and is synchronized with the picture.

Sound is recorded onto either quarter-inch tape or audio cassette. The better the quality of the tape recorder and magnetic stock, the better the quality of the sound recording. The original recording is then transferred to 16 mm or 35 mm magnetic tape that is sprocketed to match the film frames of the image. This sprocketed magnetic track makes it easy to edit the sound track and sync it with the image frame by frame.

Sometimes in animation it is useful to record the soundtrack before the artwork is made. For instance, if animated characters are to talk in lip sync, the voice tracks should be prerecorded. They are then "read"—that is, analyzed on a sound head frame by frame. Each syllable of each word can be counted in frames. The whole track analysis is written out on bar sheets, which indicate what sounds are heard for every frame of film. The exact frame counts for all of the lip sync animation are derived from the bar sheets, and the action and timing of the artwork can be planned accordingly. When the pencil test is shot, it can be viewed with the sound track, so that the movement as well as the lip sync can be judged at this stage (see Figure 2.9).

Sometimes, postscoring to picture is more suitable. In this case, the image guides the creation of the soundtrack. The selection of music or the placement of sound effects is determined by the action of the animation.

Different components of a soundtrack are

2.9 The bar sheet is used to "read" the sound track and to break each sound and syllable into frames.

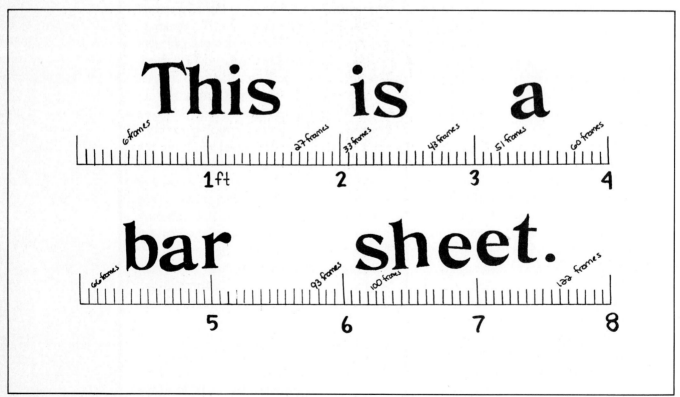

2.10

recorded onto different pieces of magnetic tape or "mag track," depending on the kinds of sounds being used. Music may be recorded onto one track and sound effects onto another. If there is more than one voice, each one may be recorded onto a separate soundtrack. Each separate track is duplicated onto magnetic film stock and individually edited and synchronized with the picture. Where there is no sound during a part of these tracks, blank stock, called "slug," is inserted so that sync is maintained throughout the full length of the film. When all the tracks have been recorded and edited, they are mixed together in a mixing studio, where volume control and sound quality balancing is possible. The sound mix enables the precise control of sound quality and volume of the individual sounds, as well as overlapping and combining of the multiple tracks onto one final mixed track. The sound mix is often done as the film is being projected in order to achieve the optimal interaction between sound and picture as the final track is being laid down.

testing

Once the format and film stock have been selected, the artwork has been framed and focused, the lighting has been set, and the F-stop determined, the shooting is ready to proceed. However, since the animation filming can be a very time-consuming and exacting task, it is useful to shoot preliminary tests to ensure that the expected results will be achieved in the final shoot.

Even though the light meter is used to read the light and set the aperture, it is a good idea to shoot exposure tests of different scenes before embarking on the final shoot. In backlit artwork, it is difficult to read the correct exposure with a light meter because each F-stop produces a different color saturation of the artwork on film. The best way to select the proper exposure setting is to shoot a test.

Exposure tests are made by shooting one frame for each F-stop and changing the setting at intervals of half-stops. These tests are known as "sinex" or "wedge" tests. When the film is pro-

52

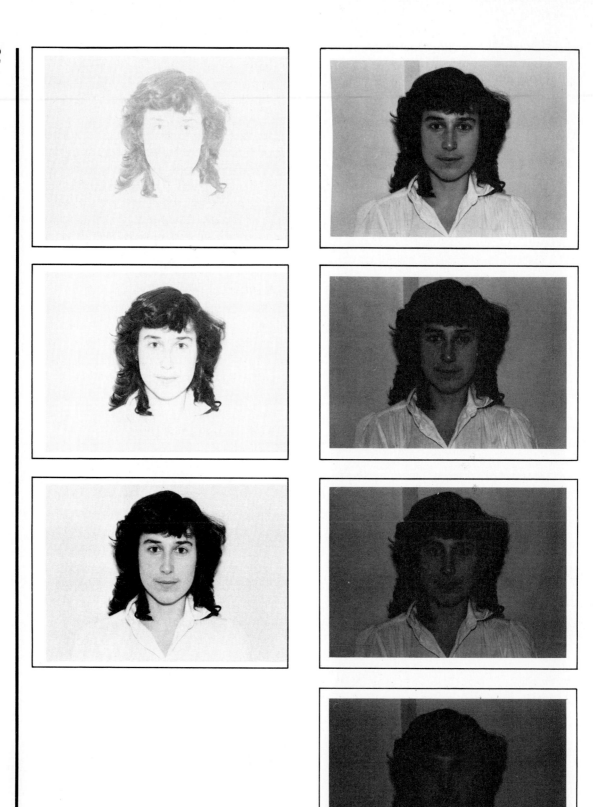

2.11 Sinex or wedge test to determine proper exposure. The bottom photo in the left column indicates correct F-stop setting.

cessed, these tests can be examined frame by frame on a light table with a loupe or magnifying glass. In this way, the exact F-stop can be selected to produce a predictable and desirable exposure (see Figure 2.11).

Motion tests, also known as pencil tests, are useful to preview animation before the artwork is finalized. The animation is done with pencil on paper before the acetates are inked and painted in cel animation, and before the Kodaliths are made and gelled in backlit animation. These pencil drawings are filmed on black and white film and projected so that any problems in the flow and style of the animation can be detected and corrected. It is well worthwhile to detect such problems in a pencil test stage, while it is still relatively easy to make adjustments in the artwork.

Knowing that the exposure and movement will work can be a reassuring factor as the final artwork and shooting are being carried out.

shooting animation

When the artwork is completed, the final shooting begins. The animation is framed and focused, and the F-stop is set according to the light meter reading and exposure tests. The camera instructions are written out on exposure sheets, which indicate the artwork and camera positioning for every frame. With accurate exposure sheets, the animation may be turned over to a professional cameraman, or else the animator may choose to shoot his or her own artwork, particularly if aesthetic decisions are going to be made as the shooting is in progress (see Figure 2.12).

2.12 Standard blank exposure sheet. Exposure sheets provide the cameraman with instructions for every level of artwork for every frame of film.

SCENE	PROJECT NO	ANIMATOR	DIRECTOR	CHECKING	BKGDS	FIELDS	FOOTAGE	SHEET

INSTRUCTION NOTES

ACTION	4	3	2	1	BKG.	FR./DIAL	ZOOM	PAN N-S	PAN E-W	CAMERA INSTRUCTIONS
						1				
						2				
						3				
						4				
						5				
						6				
						7				
						8				
						9				
						0				
						1				
						2				
						3				
						4				
						5				
						6				

54

Shooting animation requires patience and precision. Sometimes, setting up for one frame may take several minutes or more. As there are 24 frames per second, the amount of shooting time may take many hours or even days, and the resulting projected image may last only a few seconds.

Animation camerawork can be extremely frustrating. For instance, after hours of shooting fifteen or twenty passes to create one scene, a single mistake may require starting over again. On the other hand, some people find it a creative task and develop their own style and shooting rhythms that make the process innovative and enjoyable. In any case, animation must be shot deliberately and precisely to produce the final film as intended.

editing

Editing is that part of the filmmaking process in which the final form of the film is evolved and assembled sequence by sequence to the exact frame. When the shooting is completed, the film is sent to the lab to be processed. This piece of film is called the camera original, or the camera negative. To preserve its quality, whether it is reversal or negative stock, a print of the original is made as soon as the film has been developed. This print is known as the workprint, and it is used for screening and editing work. To avoid scratches and dirt, the camera original is never projected, and once the workprint has been struck, the original is put aside until the editorial work is complete.

Often, a great deal of preplanning goes into art production for animation, and thus there is little editorial work to be done once the film has been shot. But changes may be made, bad frames may be cut out, and various pieces of film may be spliced together in the editorial stage.

In order to properly "see" the film, it should be projected onto a large screen when editorial judgments are being made. The small viewing screen of a Moviola or editing viewer does not provide a true version of how the film actually works as a projected image.

An editorial setup can be assembled with a few simple pieces of equipment. Rewinds are necessary to hold the filmreels as they are wound forward and backward. A viewer has a small screen on which the image can be seen. A squawk box is an amplifier/speaker for magnetic sound tracks. A synchronizer is designed to lock multiple picture and sound tracks into frame-by-frame sync. The film and sound sprocket holes are held by rollers and hinged arms. One of these arms can be equipped with a magnetic sound head, which is attached to the squawk box, so that the film and track can be run in sync through the synchronizer. The film goes through the viewer in order that it can be seen. The sound passes by the sound head and can be heard over the squawk box. A splicer is used to make desired cuts in both the film and the sound (see Figures 2.13, 2.14, and 2.15).

Preassembled commercially available equivalents of this setup are the flatbed and the upright editing machines. Some manufacturers of flatbed editing tables are Steenbeck and Kem. The most common upright editor is the Moviola. These machines are motorized to run the film and the sound forward and backward in sync at normal speed (see Figures 2.16 and 2.17).

Certain supplies are necessary in editorial work. Splicing tape is used with the splicer to join two pieces of film together. A grease pencil is useful in marking frames to be edited. Editing gloves are used to avoid getting fingerprints on the film. A number of plastic cores provide a convenient way of holding separate pieces of film while editorial work is in progress. A core is a small, plastic, cylindrical object around which film can be wound and stored. Trim bins are also useful for holding pieces of film. They provide space to hang and label various shots before they are cut into the film (see Figure 2.18).

The first step in editing the film is known as the rough cut. Once the order of the shots has been decided, they are spliced together end to end in sequence, leaving any extra footage at the head and tail of each shot. The rough cut can be made using single splices—that is, splices taped on only one side. It is easier to remove single splices

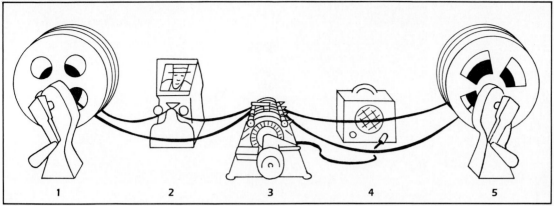

2.13

2.14

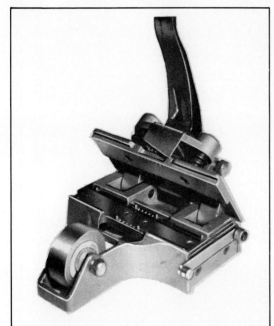

2.15

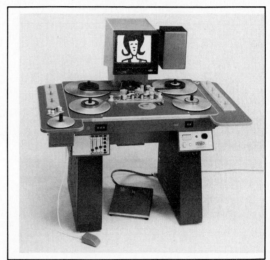

2.16

2.13 Tabletop editing setup, including (1) rewinds, (2) viewer, (3) synchronizer, (4) squawk box.

2.14 16 mm synchronizer, or "sync block," used for editing synchronized film elements. Counter in front measures footage. Numbered dial counts individual frames within one foot (1 through 40). Photo courtesy of Camera Mart, Inc.

2.15 Tape splicer.
Photo courtesy of Camera Mart, Inc.

2.16 Flatbed editing table. Film and soundtrack are run together in sync. Image is seen on viewing screen. Sound is heard through the speaker next to the viewing screen. Photo courtesy of Camera Mart, Inc.

2.17

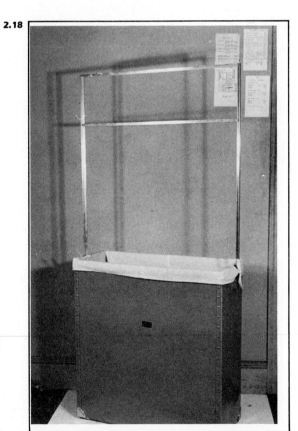

2.18

2.17 A man examines a row of upright Moviola editing machines. Viewing screen protrudes forward. Footage counter is visible to the left of the viewing screen. Separate foot pedals for image and soundtrack can be used to operate the Moviola. Photo courtesy of Camera Mart, Inc.

2.18 Trim bin for hanging and organizing pieces of film during editing. Photo courtesy of Camera Mart, Inc.

2.19

A ROLL   B ROLL

when the editing is being fine-tuned. The rough cut should be projected on a large screen repeatedly to be properly evaluated.

The next step is the <u>fine cut</u> of the film. In this process, the film is edited to the precise frame, and the splices are taped on both sides of the film. Each of the soundtracks is also fine cut in sync with the picture.

Once the tracks are all edited, the sound can be mixed while the edited picture is projected. The film is now complete in <u>interlock</u> form—that is, the sound and picture are completed on separate pieces of stock and ready to be married.

At this time, the camera original must be made to conform to the workprint. This is done using cement splices rather than tape splices. Both the original and the workprint have corresponding edge numbers printed along their edges. These edge numbers make it easy to match the original with the edited workprint.

In 16 mm film, cement splices overlap part of one frame and are therefore visible when projected. To create invisible splices, the negative is conformed to the workprint in a process called <u>A and B rolling</u>. The A-roll has shots one, three, five, and so on interconnected by black leader. The B-roll has the alternate shots two, four, six, and so on also intercut with black leader. Thus the two rolls remain in perfect sync with each other and with the workprint and sound track. When they are printed onto one piece of film, the checkerboard technique makes the cuts invisible (see Figure 2.19).

In 35 mm film, the splices fall entirely between frames and therefore do not show. It is not necessary to use A and B rolling when cutting 35 mm negative.

2.19 A and B roll checkerboard editing technique for cement splicing 16 mm camera original to prepare for answer print. A and B rolling makes splices invisible in final print.

Once the negative has been conformed, the sound and picture are composited onto one print known as the <u>answer print</u>. The mixed magnetic sound track is first printed as an <u>optical sound track</u>. The optical track is a very thin photographic line that runs along the edge of the film and changes in pattern and width. It is analyzed by a light beam in the sound head on the projector and converted into sound waves, which reach us via the projector speaker. The optical track and camera negative are composited by the film laboratory (see Figure 2.20).

The first answer print is screened to make sure the sync is correct and the color reproduction is accurate. If necessary, the lab may make slight color adjustments with filters in a process known as <u>color correction,</u> or <u>timing</u>. Once a suitably timed answer print is made, all additional prints are struck using the same timing. These prints are known as <u>release prints</u>.

the laboratory

There are several other roles besides color correction that the film lab plays in the creation of a film. Fades and dissolves can be added in the lab if they were not shot in the camera. The lab can create blow-ups and reductions from one format to another. In shooting situations where there is not enough light, the lab can "<u>push</u>" the film, that is, develop it longer than normal to bring out as much as possible in a dark image. Pushing tends to increase the graininess and contrast of the image. The lab can also "<u>flash</u>" film. Pre-flashing means exposing the unexposed raw stock to light briefly before it is shot, and post-flashing means exposing the unprocessed film to light briefly before it is developed, in an attempt to bring up a low-light exposure. Pushing and flashing are generally not necessary in animation, where lighting is easily controlled, but they may be used to create a special "look" or image quality. If footage has been torn or

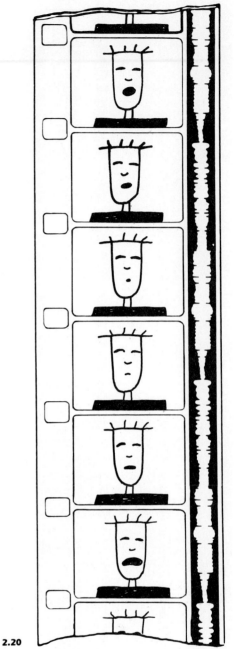

2.20

2.20 Enlarged drawing of a section of 16 mm film showing optical sound track running along the right edge.

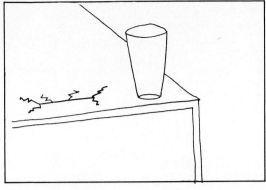

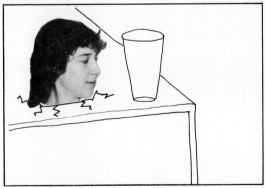

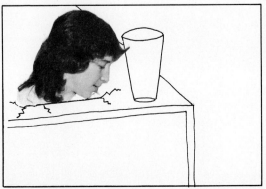

scratched, the lab has several rejuvenation processes to restore it as much as possible. One such method is known as "liquid gate" cleaning, a technique which cleans the film with a substance which fills in scratched areas in an attempt to minimize them.

The laboratory can provide information and special services which may be important in completing a film. It is a good idea to establish a relationship with the people in a film lab, because often they may have suggestions and answers to questions that can greatly effect a film production.

The preceding sections have described the stages involved in producing a finished film. They may serve as a guide from beginning to end, but most likely, at every step, there are important questions and details which will be encountered only when the filmmaker is actually going through the process. The second time around, new problems will arise and new information will be sought. Filmmaking is an ongoing learning process, from idea through final execution, and no two productions are ever the same. It takes experimentation, testing, and many mistakes to begin to master the art and the craft.

independent
animation

62

Now that we have investigated the technical areas of animated filmmaking, let us address the purposes that our films may serve. Animation is a means of communication. The production of an animated film and its eventual projection to an audience implies an idea, a message, or a point that is to be conveyed. Applications of animation include entertainment, advertisement, education, and scientific study.

The development of animation in the latter part of the nineteenth century followed several paths. In early animated films, the mere suggestion of movement was novel enough to be an end in itself, and animation quickly caught on as a form of popular entertainment. In 1914 Winsor McKay made "Gertie the Dinosaur" as part of a vaudeville stage act. The sheer novelty of the illusion of moving drawings was enough to fascinate his audiences.

Animation was also used in scientific investigation because of its ability to synthesize single images into a continuous flow of movement as well as to break down a motion into its component parts. In the 1880s, Eadweard Muybridge developed a system of photographing animals in successive stages of motion. These series of images were projected as well as published as still photographs.

Today animation is being created in greater volume for a variety of purposes. Animated feature films and cartoons are still a popular form of entertainment. Animation is used as an educational medium to illustrate and explain concepts and ideas. It is commonly found in television commercials to sell products. And it has also developed as an art form, a vehicle for personal expression.

In contrast to commercial entertainment, a number of short animated films have been independently produced by the animator as a form of self-expression. In today's economy, with the high cost of living and filmmaking, this is not often an easy pursuit. However, for some people, animation serves as a satisfying visual art form. Independent animators work in a variety of styles and techniques, depending on their preferences and interests. They may produce the entire film themselves, from conception to completion, including artwork, camera work, soundtrack, and editing. Or they may work with other people to whom they delegate certain tasks, such as shooting or sound. What sets independent animation apart from commercial animation is that the independent animator is responsible only to himself and to his intended audience. Every choice is his own, in his best attempt to design and convey whatever he wishes to express.

In the creation of an animated film, as with any film that is intended to objectify a personal point of view, it is helpful to consider several steps as the film evolves. First, the idea for the film must be clear in the filmmaker's mind, whether it be a narrative or a visually abstract idea. Next, the filmmaker must create images to populate that idea, whether they be representational or non-representational. Following this, the filmmaker should determine the structure in which the images will best convey his idea. As the filmmaking process unfolds, these three stages will begin to coalesce and interplay, each one enhancing the others. But it is important that the images and the structure of the film support the idea of the film at all times because the idea is essentially the reason for making the film.

The understanding of this process is a very difficult one. It can take many years and many films before the filmmaker begins to master his craft technically as well as conceptually. Even in the beginning stages, it is useful to be conscious of how the many creative choices that go into the production of a film can be handled with some degree of order and deliberateness.

funding
Animation is a relatively adaptable medium for an artist. A film can be made with inexpensive materials as simple as a stack of white paper and a pencil. It does not require a large amount of work space or a studio with ideal lighting. Animated drawings can be made anywhere—if necessary, with a portable light table. If shooting space is required for a three-dimensional animation setup, or if an area is required for

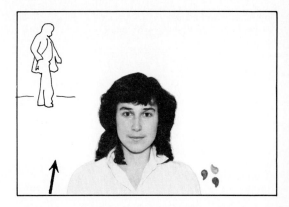
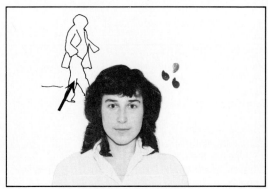
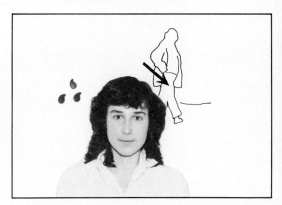
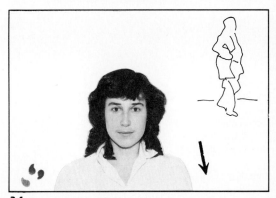

laying out sequences of painted cels to dry, one corner of a room in an apartment can serve the purpose temporarily. Lighting and camera equipment can be rented by the day or borrowed for a short time. Often, the longest period of time in the production of an animated film is spent on art production, whereas shooting may take only a few days.

It is not difficult or expensive to design a home-made animation stand, using a tripod or copy stand, or constructing one out of wood or metal. A group of animators may wish to pool their resources and share space and equipment to make their own films.

Ideally, with an unlimited budget, an animator could set up a studio equipped with all the supplies and equipment he might need or want. He could buy or rent time on an Oxberry to shoot his film, and he could create his sound-track in a professional recording and mixing studio. He could shoot his film on 35 mm stock, and when it was finished, he could arrange for special theater screenings. For an independent animation artist, these things are luxuries and not necessary for the production of a good film. It is the creativity of the animator in both his conception and execution that enables him to complete the film he has set out to make.

As in the other arts, independent animators solve the problem of funding their work in a number of ways. Some animators have independent sources of funds that they use to make their films. It is also possible to receive grants from foundations such as the American Film Institute, the National Endowment for the Arts, or the Guggenheim Foundation, which support filmmakers and other artists for specific projects. Grants may range from several hundred dollars to several hundreds of thousand dollars, depending on the nature of the foundation and the budget of the proposed film. Grant-giving is a highly selective process, and in times of a tight

3.1 Photograph, rotoscope, and rubber stamps.

64

economy, funding for projects in the arts tends to diminish. But with time, research, and a worthy proposal, it is possible to obtain full or partial support for a film project from such institutions. These resources can be found in such books as The Foundation Directory and The Annual Registry of Grants, which are available in public libraries.

The independent animator may find a job to support his artwork. Some animators work in animation studios, using their skills professionally. Others teach animation in high schools and universities that offer film courses. Some animators prefer not to work in an animation-related field. They may work in a restaurant or office doing something completely different from their own artwork.

The biggest consideration in funding independent animation is the balance between the time spent acquiring money and the time spent making the film. Whether it is time spent writing grant proposals, teaching, or waiting on tables at night, it is important that each individual artist understand his own time and energy requirements for creating his own work. It is a constant struggle to structure a lifestyle that is conducive to the spiritual as well as the physical needs of creating any kind of art. Yet for the committed artist, it is a struggle worth undertaking and one that is possible to win.

screenings

Once an animated film has been completed, it is important that it take on its own life and be seen by as many people as possible. It is difficult to obtain wide theatre distribution for a short animated film, but there are circuits in which such films may be screened for wider audiences than friends and family.

Many American and foreign film festivals are either entirely devoted to animated films or have special animation categories. Most of these festivals occur annually and provide for a gathering of audiences interested in independent films and animation. A listing of some of these festivals follows:

American Film Festival
Educational Film Library Association
43 West 61st Street
New York, NY 10023

Annency International Animated Film Festival
21 Rue de la Tour D'Auvergne
75009 Paris
France

ASIFA-East Animated Film Awards
ASIFA-East
25 West 45th Street
10th Floor
New York, NY 10036

Athens International Film Festival
Box 388
Athens, Ohio 45701

International Tournée of Animation
Diamond Heights, Box 31349
San Francisco, CA 94131

Ottawa International Film Festival
Canadian Film Institute
75 Albert Street, Suite 1105
Ottawa, Ontario KIP
Canada

Sinking Creek Film Celebration
Creekside Farm
Route 8
Greeneville, TN 37743

Zagreb World Animated Film Festival
Vlaska 70
4100 Zagreb
Yugoslavia

There are, as well, a number of film exhibition centers that seek out and screen independent animation. Several such places are the following:

Anthology Film Archives
80 Wooster Street
New York, NY 10012

Center Screen
Cambridge, Mass. 02139

Film Forum
57 Watts Street
New York, NY 10013

Millenium Film Workshop
66 East 4th Street
New York, NY 10003

Museum of Modern Art
21 West 53rd Street
New York, NY 10019

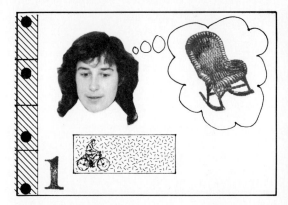

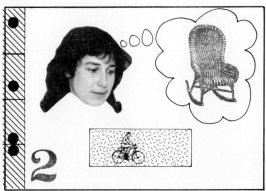

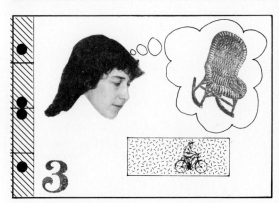

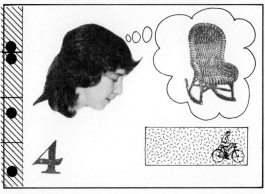

3.2

Pacific Film Archives
University Art Museum
2625 Durant Ave.
Berkeley, CA 94720

Pittsburgh Filmmakers, Inc.
P.O. Box 7200
Pittsburgh, PA 15213

Walker Art Center
Vineland Place
Minneapolis, MN 55403

Whitney Museum of American Art
945 Madison Avenue
New York, NY 10021

As the cable television market expands, there is a growing need for programming material. Cable stations are leasing and purchasing animated films for use as short subjects and fillers.

The wider the distribution of the film, the more people will have the opportunity to see it. The independent animator may elect to distribute his own work. If he wishes, however, there are a number of professional film distribution companies that handle animated films. They take the responsibility of publicizing the film, sending it to film festivals, and trying to sell or rent prints to interested parties such as schools, libraries, museums, and film societies and organizations. Although the distributor may keep up to seventy or eighty percent of any monetary intake from film sales and rentals, it is often useful to find a competent distribution company whose expertise is in having the film screened as often as possible. Different distribution companies specialize in different types of films, so it is a good idea to investigate the most suitable distributors for a specific film. A substantial list of film festivals, screening centers, and distributors may be found in Kit Laybourne's The Animation Book (Crown Publishers, New York, 1979).

group animation games
The independent animator often works alone in a small dark room, drawing for hours and hours over a light box. The work tends to be solitary and isolating.

There are, however, animation games that can be explored with a group. Perhaps a group of animators living in the same city wish to meet one night a week to animate together as a break from their own personal work. Or an animation class may want to spend class time drawing animation as a group. The interaction of the group and the interplay of individual ideas and animation offer the opportunity for people to work together and to have an exposure to different styles and attitudes.

The following games are suggestions for a group of animators working together. Each person should come with a box of 4 by 6 inch blank white index cards and drawing tools.

1. A group flip book is a flip book that grows as it is passed along through the group. Each person draws twelve successive drawings. Either all twelve or only the last one is passed to the next person, who adds twelve more drawings, and again passes either the whole stack of cards or only the last one to the next person. Any rules may be imposed. For instance, maybe one flip book dictates only the use of areas of color rather than lines. One flip book may have a character that plays an integral part in the theme. One flip book may deal with a particular theme, such as nightmares, politics, or food. Each person may choose a color and work only in that color. The colored marker may be passed along with the drawings, so that each flip book continues in its own color. A time limit may be established for each twelve drawings. The members of the group may want to bring portable light boxes, but index cards are just thin enough to see through for reference from one drawing to the next. This game produces as many flip books as there are animators in the group.

2. In the game of drawing each other the group members sit in two lines facing each other. Each person draws the person opposite him, and then changes his seat by moving one seat to the right. Again, each person draws the new person across from him, and again, seats are changed. This continues until everyone is back in his original position. Using the drawings of each person as key frames, the in-betweens are drawn, animating a transition from one drawing to the

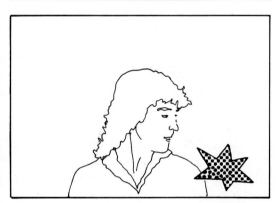

3.3

next. Each person will end up with his own animation of the members of the group.

3. One at a time, each person in the group serves as model for the rest of the group, posing in a series of animated gestures. Each model should decide on what he will enact. He may pose in a set number of positions. He may animate a cycle by his poses. He may pose with an object, or two members of the group may elect to pose together. Perhaps each model will pose in a series of positions enacting a specific emotion. The animator may wish to study one part of the body only in each pose. Again, each pose should last a specified amount of time, to be determined by the model.

4. In the twenty-four drawings exercise, everyone starts by drawing a circle on the first card. The circles should be approximately the same size and in roughly the same position on each card. In drawings one through twelve, the circle should metamorphose into something else chosen by each individual animator. Drawings thirteen through twenty-four should animate back to the circle by a different route. If the cards are filmed, they will create an ever-metamorphosing circle with a one-second beat.

Another version of this exercise is for everyone to start with the same drawing. Each person should prepare enough copies of one image for everyone in the group. Starting with the same image, each person animates twenty-four drawings. This game plays with the wide range of possible "events" originating from the same starting point.

5. If the game is to draw objects, everyone is assigned to bring an object of a specified size to the group. The objects should range from small to big, from two inches to two feet. Everyone sits in a circle. The objects are placed in the center and drawn one by one from the smallest to the largest. In order to regulate the perception of size and to give a common orientation from person to person, an arbitrary field may be indicated around the objects. Again, a time limit may be set for each drawing, and each drawing should be numbered.

When each person's drawings are filmed as a sequence, one view of a growing and changing shape is perceived. When all drawings of each object are filmed in order from around the circle of the group, the shape appears to be spinning as well as growing and changing its form.

Once everyone is seated around these objects, simulated camera activity can be drawn. One may draw a zoom in or out, a fade in or out, a pan across the subject, or a dissolve from one object to the next.

6. The group sits facing one person who holds a rectangular mirror in front of him. The mirror is moved little by little in different directions, and each person draws what he sees framed by the mirror in its different positions.

7. When Xeroxing a sequence, each member of the group prepares a twelve-frame simple sequence of animation, which he Xeroxes for everyone in the group. Each person adds some additional animation to the sequences. For the next meeting, the new sequences can be Xeroxed and further animation added. This game produces multiples of the same sequence with various additions to the animation.

8. One person writes a short story to be animated by the group. The story is broken down into sections, or paragraphs, and each person animates a given portion. The sections are filmed in order, and sound is added to reproduce the story as an animated film. The writer of the story may choose to impose certain rules on the group, such as style of animation or length of the sequence, or he may leave the animation totally up to each animator.

Although these games are designed to provide the opportunity for animators to work together, the results are often exciting, and the group may wish to work together to add sound and finish the exercises as short films. For this reason, it is well worth filming the drawings and screening the film. Further inspiration and insight can result from this. It may be interesting to tape record the sounds made by the group during the meetings for possible use as soundtrack.

the
animation
industry

70 The animation industry is devoted to work that is commissioned for commercial purposes. Three major applications of commercial animation are entertainment, education, and television advertising.

Animated cartoons, television specials, and feature films are produced for entertainment. In addition, both cartoon and graphic animation are used for titles and credits in both television and feature films.

Animation is used for educational purposes to represent graphically concepts or actions that can best be communicated visually. It can illustrate industrial demonstrations with simplicity and clarity. It can be a successful way to make theories or ideas accessible to those who are unfamiliar with them. It is used as a teaching tool for students. Animation is used in scientific and medical films to illustrate that which is not visible to the human eye, such as submicroscopic activity, functions inside the body, and events in outer space.

The television commercial industry frequently makes use of animated graphics, covering the full range of styles and techniques. Rotoscoping, motion graphics, and computer-generated animation—to cite just a few—are employed in various Levi's jeans commercials to execute their strong design concepts. The familiar Pillsbury Doughboy is brought to life by means of stop-motion animation. "Tony the Tiger," the cartoon spokesman for breakfast cereal, is created as cel animation, and integrated with live-action scenes using hand-painted traveling black mattes. Sometimes, the budgets provided to make these thirty- to sixty-second sales messages are enough to fund research and development in visual design, equipment, and technology. Sometimes the graphics themselves can be quite extraordinary, regardless of their content. Whether the commercial costs $2000 or $200,000, its potential visual strength is determined by the designer's intent, the client's requirements, and the ability to integrate the two as flexibly as possible.

The steps in making a professional animation

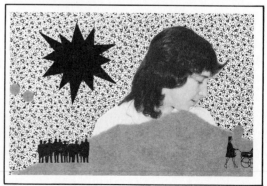

4.1

production can be exemplified by describing the production of a television commercial.

A company with a product it wishes to advertise uses the services of an advertising agency. The advertising agency generates an advertising campaign for its client, including print, radio, and television advertising, depending on the budget and needs of the company. The agency personnel work in small teams, each addressing the needs of a different client. The members of the team producing a television commercial consist of the writer, art director, producer, and account executive. The writer composes the copy for the basic concept of the commercial. The art director works from the writer's concept to create a storyboard for the visuals. The art director develops the basic look and style of the finished commercial. The agency producer coordinates the full production of the spot. He is responsible for distributing the allotted production budget and for finishing the spot on schedule. Once the production is under way, the agency producer is in constant communication with the production studio producer. The account executive in an advertising agency team is the liaison with the client. It is his responsibility to ensure that the client is informed and satisfied as the production proceeds.

In some cases, before a commercial is produced, the concept must be tested for its effectiveness. The agency will create what is called an "animatic," or a "test commercial," which is a simplified rendition of the storyboard that is usually shot from drawings of each scene on videotape. There are detailed procedures for screening an animatic for various audiences in order to evaluate its success in selling the product.

Once the concept has been sold to the client, the agency selects the company that will produce the film. Sometimes a commercial is designed to be totally animated. Sometimes, there will be only several seconds of animation incorporated in a live-action commercial, used either to demonstrate the product's action or to animate a product logo. In order to choose the most suitable production company for a particular job, the agency screens a number of sample reels from various studios. These reels provide examples of the styles and techniques in which the studio is capable of working. The selection of the production company is based on the nature of its work, its reputation, the strength of its design, budgetary considerations, scheduling requirements, and the preference of the agency's client.

the animation team

Generally, commercial animation is created by a team of people of many skills working together in various capacities. They may be employed in full-time staff positions in a production company or may be freelance professionals hired until their job is completed. Depending on the nature of the production, several roles may be filled by one person. The designer/director may also be the producer and the animator, and he may create the soundtrack for the film as well. The animator may choose to ink and paint, as well as to shoot his own animation, eliminating the need for a separate illustrator, inkers, painters, and cameraman.

In professional animation productions, however, it is common to separate the functions involved, and it is necessary to find specialists in the areas of expertise that are required in the making of an animated film.

The overall supervision, organization, and coordination of the film production is the responsibility of the producer. He is the liaison between the advertising agency and the production staff, and it is he who is first contacted by the advertising agency. The producer meets with the agency representative to discuss the proposed job, and after examining the production requirements with his designer/director, it is the producer's role to prepare and present a budget and production methodology to the advertising agency.

When a job is awarded to the production company, the producer manages all official paperwork. He signs the job contract, and he coordinates the procedures of billing, collecting, and dispensing of production funds. He must be constantly aware of the flow of money throughout the production. The paperwork may be done by a bookkeeper, but the supervision and authorization of all such work is the task of the producer.

The producer works with his designer/director to select and hire the appropriate production staff. Who should be the illustrator? How many animators are necessary? Who is the best cameraman to shoot a particular type of work? Which computer system is programmed to accommodate a chosen design?

Scheduling is another task assigned to the producer. He must devise a schedule to complete the work by the imposed deadline.

Once the production gets underway, the producer must be constantly aware of all aspects of the job to ensure that plans proceed according to budget and schedule. He arranges and attends all necessary job meetings. All approvals and decisions that are made at these meetings must be confirmed in writing by a letter from the producer to the agency.

Because of the complexities caused by so many people and the combination of so many different requirements, changes often occur and problems often arise. Frequently, a revision in the original concept will delay the schedule and involve additional work and additional costs. The producer must discuss this with the advertising agency producer to arrive at an appropriate solution. If necessary, he should make sure that any additional monies are authorized by the agency, and he must confirm all decisions that are made.

At any stage in the production, mistakes may occur. The camera may break down on the night before the film delivery deadline. The film lab may misplace the film. The animator may miscalculate the amount of time necessary to complete his job and not be able to finish on schedule. A particular color may not reproduce easily on the film stock. It is not uncommon for the agency art director to reject the first draft of the production because it does not meet his expectations. The handling of all such problems is the responsibility of the producer. He may find it necessary to hire additional assistants or to authorize overtime expenditures in order to meet the completion deadline. He may suggest changing a camera service that isn't performing properly. He must also decide whether the production is in fact acceptable according to all previous understanding, and if he feels that it is, he must stand behind it in the face of a disappointed client.

Throughout the course of the production, with all its trials and rewards, the producer must meet the needs of the advertising agency and defend the interests of his designer/director and production staff.

The designer/director is the creator of the visual and audio aspects of the film. He must integrate the client's needs with his own design skills to create a strong and aesthetic representation on film. His skills lie in adapting the original storyboard concept from the advertising agency and making it work successfully as a thirty-second film, and in understanding the proper use of graphics in animation. The designer/director determines the most suitable method for creating the image, whether it be computer animation, cel animation, backlit multipass animation, or any combination of techniques. He recommends the strongest graphic layouts, the proper structure and timing of the film, the best color selections, the use of camera moves and editing. He supervises all optical work. If the animation is to be integrated with live action in the commercial, the designer/director must discuss the full production with the live-action director in order to coordinate the animation with the live action.

All questions and decisions that arise related to the creative aspects of the production are the responsibility of the designer/director. He oversees the production to ensure the proper execution of his design. The designer/director must work closely with the producer to keep the client aware of his attitudes as they develop throughout the course of the production, so that his aesthetic standards are maintained and are evident in the final film.

A skilled illustrator has several functions in an animation studio. One of his jobs is to render the visions and concepts of the designer/director. He may be asked to illustrate a polished story-board. He may design characters and then create fully rendered models of them. He may illustrate backgrounds and props for various scenes in the film. The illustrator works as an arm of the designer/director as the visual aspects of the film evolve.

From here, the work goes to the animator and his assistant. The animator brings the illustrator's renderings to life. His skill is understanding how to animate properly to convey the intended feeling of any action. He may animate "straight ahead," drawing each frame of the sequence, or he may work on key drawings, which are the extremes of a given action and in which the essence of that action lies. The animator's work is done with pencil on numbered registered paper. This is the stage at which the intricacies of actions and movements are worked and re-worked.

Accompanying his animation, the animator includes exposure sheets, which are frame-by-frame instructions for the cameraman who will shoot the film.

The in-betweener's function is to fill in the drawings between the animator's key drawings, following the animator's style of line, movement, and characterization.

When the animation is completed, the pencil drawings are shot and the success of the animation is judged. After viewing the pencil test, the animator may make adjustments in his timing or movement. At this stage, the designer/director is able to see his concepts begin to come to life.

Once the animation is acceptable, the pencil drawings are turned over to the inkers, who carefully trace each of them with ink on acetate cels. The cels are registered exactly with the paper drawings, and numbered accordingly. Sometimes the inker's job can be replaced by Xerox techniques that transfer the pencil drawings directly onto registered cels.

These cels are delivered to the painters, or opaquers, each of whom works on a different sequence of the film. Special cel vinyl paint is applied to the flip side of the inked cels, one color at a time. All of the areas of one color are painted through the sequence. Once they have dried, another color is added to the sequence in the same fashion, until every cel is fully colored.

The role of the checker is to review the inked and painted cels before they are shot. He must make sure that all areas of color have been applied and that none of the cels is out of numerical order. He must also check the exposure sheets against the artwork for any inaccuracies. Checking ensures that there are no careless errors that will appear on the film once it is shot.

The finished animation cels are now turned over to the cameraman, who follows the animator's exposure sheets to film the animation. It is the exposure sheets that indicate to the cameraman the number and order of the cel levels, which cels are used in every frame, and the activity of the camera frame by frame. The cameraman generally shoots exposure tests of all art elements before shooting the final film. This is particularly important in the case of backlit animation, where color is determined by the amount of light hitting the film. These tests are known as sinex tests or wedge tests. The designer/director should view these tests with the cameraman and recommend proper exposure selections.

When the film has been shot, it is sent to the lab to be processed and printed. It is then delivered to the editor, who makes any necessary splices to assemble the film. Editorial work in animation is generally minimal, because the artwork is planned and essentially pre-edited before it is shot. If a sound track exists, the editor syncs up the sound and picture. He puts appropriate leader on the film and labels all the elements. The sound and image can now be screened together in interlock for the producer, designer/director, and client.

If the film is complete and acceptable, the editor works with the lab to make any additional color corrections and to make composited answer prints of the film.

The film may require optical work before it is answer printed. Opticals are costly, but if they have been covered by the budget, they are frequently used for a number of purposes in commercial animation. An optical is often preferred over in-camera bipacking for combining various film elements because it is more precise and more easily controlled than a bipack run. Opticals are used to integrate animation and mattes with existing live-action footage. Any fades, dissolves, or freeze frames that were not shot in camera can be added optically. Special effects, such as highlighting, colorizing, or glowing colors and halos can be created on an optical bench if they were not included in the original film shoot.

The editor lays out the workprints of all film elements with markings indicating what optical work is necessary. He delivers these elements and the camera original to the optical house. A film optical is done with IP (interpositive) or CRI (color reversal internegative), which is struck from the camera original. All elements to be used in opticals must be tested for correct exposure and color reproduction in a second series of sinex tests before the final optical is made. The optical negative becomes the final version of the film, and it is used to strike the answer print and release prints.

If the film is to be post-scored, the final version may be turned over to a composer who creates a soundtrack, or to a stock music house where appropriate music can be purchased. If sound effects are to be added, they may be purchased from a sound effects library, or they may be created by a sound effects specialist. Selected sound tracks are sent to the editor, who works with the designer/director to sync up all sound elements with the picture. If there is more than one track (e.g., an announcer, a musical score, and various sound effects), they are all synced up with the picture as separate rolls of magnetic stock that must then be mixed together into a single sound track. This is done by a sound mixer

at a mixing studio, which enables precise volume control as well as the ability to equalize and fine-tune all sounds. The editor, producer, designer/director, and client work with the sound mixer to reach a mutually satisfactory result.

There is sometimes a need for other kinds of specialists in an animation production. If models are to be animated, a skilled model maker will be employed to create models which can be acceptably reproduced on film. It is often a legal requirement in a television commercial that the colors of a product on film match exactly its colors in print. Since print colors are not directly translatable to film colors, any product model being shot must be color-corrected before it is filmed. This is done by slightly adjusting the colors of the product model so that their film equivalents will be the proper hue.

Because technology continues to play a greater role in animation, a technical director is occasionally a necessary part of the production. In working with computer-operated equipment, and in creating complex combinations of many different film elements, the technical director works with the designer/director to inform him of the technical possibilities available to him, and to facilitate communication between the equipment operators and the designer/director. He also assures that all technical work is understood and proceeding as intended. By doing so, he relieves the designer/director of this responsibility and frees him to concentrate on the aesthetics of the film.

The roles involved in the production of computer-generated animation are slightly different because all artwork is created and animated by the computer. The computer animator serves the functions of illustrator, animator, in-betweener, inker, painter, checker, cameraman, editor, and optical house. He must clearly understand the attitudes and ideas of the designer/director, and he must operate the computer to create the film according to the designer/director's instructions at all stages. It is important that the designer/director and the computer animator learn to understand each other's specialized language so that the fullest interaction between the film graphics and the computer's capabilities is made possible.

Testing is an important part of computer animation, and the computer animator produces motion and color tests for the client's approval. In some computer systems, these tests can be viewed directly on the computer monitor and adjustments can be made in real time. The producer, designer/director, and client can work with the computer animator until the moves and colors are mutually satisfactory.

In order to achieve the desired animation, it may be more than a question of merely adjusting certain lines or colors in a problem area; instead, an entirely different program may be necessary to fulfill the designer/director's intentions. Here, a computer programmer becomes involved in the production. After discussing the needs of the job with the computer animator, the programmer must design a program that will enable the computer animator to realize the goals of the designer/director.

At present, the cooperation of the computer experts and the film designers is progressing rapidly. The interaction between them is beginning to create a whole new range of graphic possibilities for both.

the production process

Commercial animation is a competitive business. Studios promote themselves on their individual strengths. Some are specialists in cartoon animation; others in animation graphics and design; and others in computer animation. Some studios emphasize their ability to provide fast and inexpensive productions.

It is essential that the production company exploit its capabilities and make itself known to the advertising agencies, for their mutual benefits. Advertising in commercial trade publications is a useful investment for a company. A strong

sample reel is also important, because it represents the company's potential. The sample reel, usually a 3/4-inch video cassette, serves as a portfolio of its production abilities. A sales representative will often distribute the sample reel to advertising agencies and other potential clients in order to expose the company's name and products as widely as possible.

Once the advertising agency has approval on a storyboard for a commercial, the bidding process begins. The agency producer distributes the storyboard and production requirements to the producers of several different animation companies to obtain competitive cost proposals. Agencies often follow the standard three-bid system, in which three peer group companies are bid. Sometimes, however, there are single-bid situations, in which if the price is acceptable, the job is awarded on the basis of one bid. There are also occasions when storyboards are given to five or six production companies that specialize in different techniques and budget ranges (see Figure 4.2).

Besides the storyboard, the specific production requirements for a job are delineated in a specification sheet. The "spec sheet" includes the name of the agency, the client, the product, the agency personnel, and sometimes the names of the other competing companies. It specifies the length of the commercial and the scheduled delivery date, and it indicates what the agency intends to supply for the production. The spec sheet indicates what the production company should cover in its budget. The agency generally provides the actual advertised product, clean artwork for logos and labels when necessary, and proper color requirements for product and logo reproduction. The agency may provide a mixed sound track, or it may ask that the production company supply sound effects and final mix of the sound track. The spec sheet states whether the agency wishes the production company to budget for a film-to-tape transfer when the spot is complete. It lists the contractual deliverables, such as additional 35 mm prints, 16 mm answer prints, and 3/4-inch video cassettes. All the items required of the produc-

Audio
MOM: How can I keep my kids' clothes
clean??

Audio
SPOKESMAN: You should be using LUX-O,
the only way to get your wash really
clean every time.

4.2 The storyboard visually describes the concept of
the commercial. It is prepared by the art director at the
advertising agency and distributed to the production
companies who are being bid for the job. The
production companies use it as a basis to evaluate the
creative and technical requirements of the
production, in order to arrive at a proper bidding price.

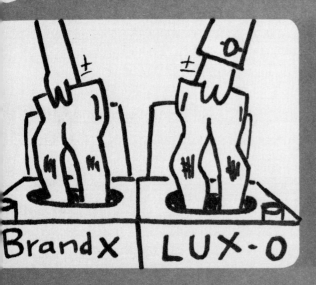

Audio
SPOKESMAN: Compare LUX-O with the
   leading Brand X.

Audio
SPOKESMAN: Discover the LUX-O difference
   It'll make your wash sparkle!

Production Co.:	Bid Date:	Actualization Date:
Address:	Client:	Agency Job No.:
Telephone No.:	Product:	
Production Contact:	Agency:	
Director:	Agency Producer:	Tel:
Designer:	Agency Art Director:	Tel:
Editor:	Agency Writer:	Tel:
Other:	Agency Bus. Mgr.:	Tel:

CONTRACT REQUIREMENTS	Code No.	Commercial Title
35mm prints	1.	
16mm prints	2.	
Videotape Dubs	3.	
3/4" Cassettes	Color VTR 35mm 16mm Completion Date	

REQUIREMENTS AGENCY CONTRACTOR   REQUIREMENTS AGENCY CONTRACTOR

Talent	Product
Casting	Props
Make Up/Hair	Stock Footage
Wardrobe	Stylist
Soundtrack: Voice Over	Artwork
Sound Effects	Editorial
Music:Original	Animation
Music:Stock	Titles
Final Mixed Track	Film to 2" VTR Transfer

SUMMARY OF PRODUCTION COSTS	ESTIMATED	ACTUAL
1. Pre-production and wrap costs		
2. Shooting crew labor		
3. Location and travel expenses		
4. Props, wardrobe, animals		
5. Studio and set construction costs		
6. Equipment costs		
7. Film stock No. feet mm		
8. Miscellaneous		
9. Sub Total		
10. Director/Creative fees		
11. Insurance		
12. Sub Total		
13. Production fee		
14. Talent costs and expenses		
15. Editorial and finishing		
16.		
17. Grand Total		
18. Contingency		

COMMENTS

4.3 Example of a commercial bid and spec sheet. It is partially filled in by the advertising agency and presented to the production company. The production company completes the form and returns it to the agency with its formal bid.

tion company must be included in the bid submitted to the agency (see Figure 4.3).

A bidders' information conference may take place in an open session, where producers from each animation company are called into the advertising agency at the same time. The agency producer explains the board and job specifications at this meeting and answers any questions that may arise. Each producer takes the board back to his office and submits his bid after evaluating the job.

A closed session occurs when the agency producer sets individual appointments with the producers from each candidate studio and discusses the job on a private basis. Again, bids are presented at a later date.

Sometimes all bidding information is communicated by telephone, particularly when the agency and production company are located in different cities.

During the next several days, the producer evaluates the best approach to the job and the requirements of the production in terms of materials, time, labor, and equipment. He calculates his overhead and profit margin in arriving at a price. The acceptable standard markup for commercial productions is 35 percent. He must also consider his competitors, in order to determine a profitable, yet competitive, production bid.

The initial price and production description are called in by telephone to the agency producer. This is generally followed up by a written bid. Some agencies will supply bid forms that the production company must fill out in making an official bid. Otherwise, the bid is submitted in letter form. It may simply confirm the telephone price, or it may be more extensive, providing a full design and production methodology, an itemized budget breakdown of all aspects of the production, and a tentative production schedule.

If the production deadline is unusually demanding, two bids may be submitted. One price cov-

ers a normal production, the second an overtime budget to ensure that the agency's schedule is met. Even though the overtime budget is higher, production companies generally prefer to work on a normal schedule, because the quality of the work tends to be higher when proper working time is available. Sometimes an agency will postpone its deadline when unforeseen problems arise. However, if there is a confirmed purchase of expensive air time, it may be necessary to enter into an overtime agreement.

In some cases, the agency may request design input from the animation studio. It may ask an animation designer to create a logo treatment for the product. The art director may have ideas for a storyboard, but he may invite creative feedback from a designer/director who has a better knowledge of the aesthetic and technical workings of animation. Sometimes the agency may supply copy to the production company and ask for storyboard designs. In these situations, the production company may ask for a separate design fee to cover the cost of storyboard production and creative input. Once the design has been approved, a budget is submitted to cover the production costs. Occasionally, this design fee is added to the production budget if the storyboard is approved. Otherwise, it is a separate fee that is paid regardless of whether the design is actually produced.

Following are examples of budget categories for different methods of animation production.

For cel animation

Designer/director
Storyboard and layout
Production expenses and materials
Color models
Background illustration
Animator
Assistant animator
In-betweener
Inkers and painters
Airbrushing
Camera: pencil test
Camera: final shooting
Stock and processing
Editorial
35 percent markup
Total

For motion graphic animation

Designer/director
Layout
Art preparation
Kodaliths and stats
Production expenses and material
Animator
Assistant animator
Matte painting
Camera: sinex and motion tests
Camera: mattes
Camera: final shooting
Stock and processing
Editorial
35 percent markup
Total

For rotoscoping combined with existing live action

Designer/director
Production expenses and material
Art preparation
Kodaliths and stats
Animator
Assistant animator
Matte painting
Camera: rotoscoping
Camera: sinex and motion tests
Camera: mattes
Camera: final shooting
Stock and processing
Editorial and layout for opticals
Opticals
35 percent markup
Total

For stop-motion animation

Designer/director
Model making
Set and props
Stop-motion rigging
Stop-motion photography: testing
Stop-motion photography: final
Equipment rental
Stock and processing
Editorial
35 percent markup
Total

Additonal items that may be required in a production budget are:

Sound effects
Sound mix
Videotape transfer
16 mm contract prints
Travel expenses

Computer animation is often budgeted according to the number of seconds of animation necessary.

If a production is technically unusual or experimental, the production company may request that a contingency be set aside should the production run into unexpected difficulties. This contingency is usually a percentage of the production budget, and it is not used unless the production company finds that the agency's requirements cannot be met in the original budget. The agency must then obtain authorization from its client to make use of the contingency fee.

When the advertising agency producer has collected final bids from each production company, he submits them to the client, and a decision is made as to which company will be awarded the job. Sometimes this decision is based on which company presents the lowest bid. This is not, however, always the deciding factor. Selection may be based on production methodology, examples of the production company's work, location of the production company, and the ability to produce the job on schedule. In some cases, the agency producer may have had previous experience with a particular studio and may elect to maintain a working relationship that has proven successful in the past. In the final analysis, an award is based as much on a company's ability and past performance as on its budget.

The agency producer contacts the production company producer to inform him that his bid has been accepted. At this point, there is an exchange of paper work that officially authorizes the production. The agency supplies the production company with a purchase order indicating that the full production budget has been allocated to them. The purchase order may also serve as a contract between the agency and the studio. In some cases, a separate contract is drawn up, reiterating price and production requirements, and signed by authorized representatives from both the agency and the production company. The contract also states the billing procedure and payment schedule for the production. Sometimes the production company receives 50 percent of the production in advance, and 50 percent when the job is delivered. Or payments may be made in three installments, the first when the job is awarded, the second when all tests have been approved, and the third when the final job is delivered and accepted. These installments may be made as payments of 50 percent, 25 percent, 25 percent, or 33 percent, 33 percent, 33 percent, and in some cases, 50 percent, 40 percent, 10 percent, depending on the policies of both the advertising agency and the production company. As soon as the job has been awarded, the production company submits an invoice for the first payment.

To put the job in motion, a production meeting is arranged so that everyone involved can meet and discuss the assignment. The agency team, including the producer, art director, writer, and account executive, and the producer and designer/director from the production company, are present. Depending on the nature of the job, any other key figures in the production, such as the live-action director, the computer animator, a special illustrator, or model maker may attend to ensure that everyone has a clear understanding of all aspects of the job. The meeting provides an opportunity to discuss all aspects of the production so that the final commercial meets all the requirements of the agency.

A production schedule is evolved once the requirements of the production have been fully clarified. Throughout the job, there are various stages at which agency approval is required before continuing the production. The schedule indicates at what points these approvals will be sought, so that the agency and client can plan to be available.

Each production has its own specific scheduling needs, but frequently, the time allotted for production of a 30-second animated spot is six to eight weeks. Sometimes the agency will require the finished commercial in four to five weeks, and this may determine its style and production value. On occasion, for more involved jobs, a 10- to 12-week schedule is possible.

Following is a general schedule structure that various animation jobs may follow.

Layout and color models	1 to 2 weeks
Product model for stop motion	3 to 4 weeks
Sinex and exposure tests	3 to 4 weeks
Motion tests	4 to 5 weeks
Rough cut or pre-optical screening	6 to 7 weeks
Final optical interlock screening	7 to 10 weeks
Sound effects and final mix	7 to 10 weeks
Video tape transfers	7 to 10 weeks

It is anticipated that the job will proceed according to schedule and that the final deadline will be met. However, a number of problems may be encountered that could effect the flow of the production.

Delays at any stage of approval will hold up the production process. Sometimes a key figure from the agency is not available to give approval. At times, the agency is required to send tests to an out-of-town client for approval, causing a waiting period of several days before proceeding. At each approval point, if significant problems or changes arise, the original schedule can be effected. It is essential that both the agency and the production company be aware of the final deadline, and that the effect of delays or changes on the schedule be understood by the agency. The responsibility for delays that occur due to the agency or client must be accepted by the agency. The number of days lost at each stage can legitimately delay the delivery date of the film by an equal number of days. If a delay is not acceptable, the agency may be required to pay additional overtime money to ensure that the film is completed on time.

If the agency revises the original concept in the middle of the production, the production company may request additional time and/or money to accommodate such changes.

On the other hand, it is unlikely that the production of the film will proceed without problems and errors. The stringent and exact requirements of animation often result in more than one attempt before the exposures, animation movements, camera work, bipacking, or opticals are correct. These difficulties can, one hopes, be anticipated and enough time for adjustments can be built into the production schedule. However, the cost of such mistakes and the responsibility for reshooting and remaking is the production company's.

As carefully as a job may be discussed and

82

planned, the finished film may not always be satisfactory. Sometimes the film does not meet the expectations of the agency or the client. Sometimes the production company may overestimate its abilities, and the final film falls short of the desired goal. At this point, it may be too late to remake the film. The agency and production company must negotiate a satisfactory solution. The film may be acceptable even if it is not perfect. The agency may choose to use the imperfect spot until the production company delivers a corrected version, or the agency may decide that the film is completely unusable, and may threaten not to pay the production company the final payment. The more communication there has been throughout the production, the easier it is to understand and settle such a difficult situation. It may be unclear as to where the blame actually lies and what, if anything, can be done to correct it. At this point, lawyers may be called in to settle the differences or to negotiate a financial arrangement.

Usually the final film is finished on schedule, and the agency and client are pleased with the results. Once the completed spot has been approved, the production company submits its invoice for final payment. It is important for the production company to obtain a print or video-tape of the commercial to include in its library.

Clear, open communication and reciprocal understanding between the advertising agency and the production company usually result in fewer errors and a smoother production. This is to the advantage of both parties. The agency receives a better film and maintains a healthy relationship with its client. The production company produces a better film to show as an example of its work. At the same time, it establishes a good rapport with its client, which may result in continued business.

the
interviews

84 The preceding sections have described the various aspects of the art of animation production. To appreciate this more fully, I decided to discuss with various professionals the roles they play and the experiences they have had in making successful animated films.

Following is a series of interviews with individuals who work in various positions in the field of animation. The interviews attempt to cover a description of what these people do in their current positions, what in their backgrounds have led them to this work, and their attitude toward what they do. Interestingly, each person's story is unique. Their ages range from 25 to 65 years, and their histories and goals point out the wide range of personalities working in the field. Not every position in animation is covered here, and some people play more than one role in the production of an animated film. These interviews provide an inside view of the different aspects of the animation field, based on the direct experience of those working in these roles. Because I live in New York City, most of the people interviewed live and work there, and are associated with the advertising industry rather than the feature film industry.

harold friedman: producer

My role as a producer is similar to that of a producer in Hollywood on a feature film in that I combine the elements of making the production a reality. Now, as it pertains to my particular skill and specialty, which is commercials, it takes on other meanings. In the commercials business, in order to become a producer, you first have to have a job to produce. And therefore, you have to solicit the account through the advertising agency. You have to make them aware of the body of work of the designer/directors they might be interested in working with. When the agency has seen the work of a designer/director or illustrator who particularly satisfies their needs, they then advise me that they are interested in doing a production and present a storyboard. A storyboard is a visualization with copy of how they conceive an idea of what would make their product sell, and of how they wish to

5.1

present that idea filmically, whether it be cartoon animation, motion graphics, or a combination of live action and special effects. Once we have gone through the understanding of what it is that they expect, we then take the storyboard and discuss with the designer/director the requirements of the agency. The designer/director evaluates the storyboard and develops a production attitude and methodology. Working with the designer/director, we develop a budget encompassing all of the elements, showing how much is allocated for the designer/director, how much is allocated for the animation, how much is allocated for the camera, how much is allocated for artwork, backgrounds, in-betweens, stand work, lab work, editorial and optical phases—everything that is concerned with the actual production costs. We in turn present the budget, along with the design attitude for the production, to the agency. Thus, we have submitted our bid.

Generally, the agencies work with a three-bid system. In other words, three competitive companies will be asked to submit bids on the same job. We feel it is important that the three companies are, indeed, on a peer group level, so that the production values that we indicate we will develop in doing a particular production will reasonably reflect what our competitors will do. Even though they may come up with different production attitudes, the three bids should reasonably be within a 10 percent range of one another.

When we are awarded a job, there may be several deciding factors. The agency may wish to work with the particular designer/director we have suggested. Perhaps they have worked with him previously and wish to maintain a continuity of relationship. Or perhaps they are looking for new talent and are particularly impressed by his work. The agency may also choose to work with me as producer, and with my company because they feel we can fulfill their needs in delivering their job both well done and on time for their airdate.

In any case, once we have won the award, we proceed to make the commercial. First of all, we have a production meeting. The designer/director, the producer, and the agency personnel, including the producer on their part, the creative supervisor, the writer, the art director, and the account person, all meet to discuss their mutual objectives in the production, in order to turn out an excellent commercial that will satisfy the people involved, meaning the agency team, the designer/director who is the creative person, plus ourselves as producers. We hope to produce a commercial so good that we can put it on our reel as an example of the kind of work we do and the excellence of the people involved. Then, we hope, it is that good that it goes on to win prizes. In addition to the prizes, it is important that it come out profitably for all of us, and that it begets additional work because it is recognized as a well made, effective commercial.

We've had several examples of this. We started with a "Bubblicious" chewing gum commercial, and now we've done six of them with the same agency. The styles have evolved from commercial to commercial; the designer/directors have changed because of availability and differences in attitude; and the agency personnel have changed. The excellence of our production value and the seriousness of our professionalism in turning out high quality product and understanding the objectives of the commercials are part of the reason that we were awarded these commercials time and time again.

The producer must have an understanding of the client as well as the creative talents involved in the production. He must have a thorough knowledge of what is to be achieved in order to coordinate the production and make it all come together within a schedule at a profit.

The commercial goes out to a huge public. At best, it should meet the designer/director's creative and technical standards as well as fulfill the client's marketing strategies. It must also be produced within a given time schedule so that the client can purchase costly air time and feel secure that his commercial will be ready. The ability to produce these elements, to make it all work, and come out on time so that it makes an airdate is a skill that is developed over a period of time of understanding the requirements of the people involved.

I have been a business type since I was a child. I understand the business of business. Turning out something at a profit is something I've known about for a long time. Turning it out well is a skill that I continually develop as my knowledge increases. I come from the music business, and I've always been in tune to sound. In animation, the motivation of the picture often starts with the sound track. How exciting is it? How does it relate to the subject material? Visuals are created that are in sync with and inspired by the sound track. At the same time, the visuals can motivate the makers of the sound so that they can come back and, as we term it in the industry, sweeten the existing track after seeing the image. The sound and music person can supplement and amplify what was done with the sound to begin with, so that the visuals and the sound become synergistic, and produce a better spot. From time to time, we produce such powerful visuals that they inspire and motivate the sound track to come up to the aspirations and the attitudes of the visuals. This is the mark of a successful and well-produced commercial. Sound is such an important element in commercials and, in particular, animation. My experience in the music business has given me a sense of what things should sound like in combination with what things should look like.

Before working in animation, I worked in live action, where I really started to learn the ins and outs of the film business. Having done that successfully, I joined a production company called Elektra, which at the time was considered the best and largest. Elektra spawned many of the great talents in our business: Lee Savage, Pablo Ferro, Freddy McGubgub, Jack Goodford, R.O. Blechman, Phil Kimmelman, Hal Silvermintz, and a host of others. This whole group was in sympathy and in competition with one another at the same time, so the results were outstanding.

A romance developed between animation and me. I enjoyed being able to exercise the controls possible in animation. The ability to make,

remake, and make it better fascinated me. For me, it was a labor of love, combining my background in live action and music. Having the skill and professionalism of a business type, I was able to get the best juices of the creative without interfering, and yet fulfill the requirement for which we were hired, which was to produce commercials. The results were exceptionally good. We were recognized as being just about the best in the business.

After working at Elektra, I became partners with Lee Savage, whom I had met there. We formed a company called Savage-Friedman. Strangely, we did practically no animation. We did live action, but it was all graphically oriented. It was peculiar, it was special, it was original, and it was all design-oriented. The reason for this is that Savage, having been an artist, designer, and animation director, applied these skills and attitudes in his live-action directing. So instead of drawing the guys with the big noses, instead of the comedic situations that were developed in our normal cel animation, our casting was in the direction of people. We hired people from "Second City" like Alan Arkin and Paul Dooley, people who were known as being strangely, uniquely individualistic, people who looked and sounded like themselves. In a sense, they were comedic characters who could almost be animated characters. Savage and I stayed together for five years. We had a very successful company. Then we split up, and I formed the Consortium based on the idea of working with skillful and talented designer/directors, each of whom was special and unique in how he or she approached a design problem and executed a concept. They were all well-known people, like Milton Glaser and Arnie Levin, who already had done a body of commercials and had a reel. The Consortium presented their work as a way of saying "Arnie Levin, Lee Savage, Mort Goldsholl, Pablo Ferro . . . this is what they look like." If the client felt that a certain designer/director could execute the commercial that they had conceived in the storyboard form, that was the designer/director selected. I, as producer, functioned in the securing of the work, and then followed all the way to the end of the production to final delivery of the spot. The whole concept of the Consortium is that the producer is responsible for these very talented individuals who look like what they look like on their reels, and who are presented for their particular opinions, attitudes, skills, and abilities.

d. rufus friedman: producer

As producer, I put together the appropriate production team for the client. I may work with a character animator, a motion graphics animator, and a live-action director, and combine those three elements for the production. When I'm doing my best work, I serve as an effective communication link between the client and those three people.

Another area of my work is to find and develop somewhat unknown talent. Our company has a reputation strong enough so that we are able to bring in new people who we feel will be able to handle the client's needs. In these cases, again, I act as liaison between the artist and the client. I also must use my experience to ensure that the production goes ahead as planned and discussed.

My job as producer entails handling the business end of things, which is personally not my favorite part of my job. I'm much happier dealing with people as opposed to numbers, but I am capable of dealing with numbers, and I understand that dealing with budgets is quite necessary and important. That's how you pay for the people you are putting together. But, as I said, I enjoy working on the creation of the film much more than the budgeting of it.

Being a producer is like making a soup. Even though you aren't the beans, the potatoes, and the meat, you are still the one who puts the ingredients together. Then you get to taste the soup. If it tastes good, you've done well. If it tastes terrible, you've made a terrible soup. And even though you aren't the beans and the onions, you are still the creator of the soup. Sometimes this analogy saves me; sometimes it causes problems. I do tend to involve myself in the creative end of whatever I'm producing, which at times puts me in jeopardy. But I think if I'm to call myself producer of a job, I have to be willing to involve myself and to take creative risks. I'm not sure if this is normally considered part of the producer's role or not.

I'm 30 years old. I haven't been doing this forever. I'm still learning a lot. And part of this learning process is confusing. I try to be as honest to both client and artist as possible. Sometimes it works, other times it tends to be more confusing. But I think, in the final run, the clearer I am, the better it is for everyone involved. If you deal in hokum, you're going to produce hokum. And I think it's more fun to be straightforward with people. It suits me more as a person.

I was born into the film business. I'm the boss's son! No, seriously, I started working in the business when I was 15 years old as a runner in an optical house. A runner is the one they tell, hey boy, run this over to either the lab, the client, the editor, or wherever they want. You are literally running. It's a sneakers job, not a brain job. It's one step below a gofer. I got paid about 65 dollars a week at that time, plus overtime. It was a very legit job. We had to punch in and out each day. This is where I got the smell of the film business. It was the best part of being a runner—getting a sense of the essence of the business. I got the job through my father's connections. That happens a lot in the film business. It probably happens that way in any business. I'd stayed away from the film business for a while just because it was my father's business. But at age 15, I decided I could make some money, and also hang out with some pretty interesting guys who were also runners. I was the youngest one, and I'd gotten the job for the summer. But it actually marked the end of my school career. I'd never been either happy or productive in school. I saw that there was, in fact, life outside of school, and I thought it was a lot more fun.

My next job was with Len Mandelbaum as third assistant editor. There I learned how to operate a Moviola, rewinds, hot splicer. I met some nice people, and learned a little not only about film editing, but about life.

Then I went to work for Phos-Cine, where I was officially a gofer. It was there that I learned the basics of animation from Arnie Levin. I also learned about professional politics during this period.

I went on to work for Ralph Bakshi in ink and paint. I continued to gain experience in animation and in the politics of the film business. I also learned about being laid off, and about how bad it feels. I learned that I never wanted to do that to anyone if I ever found myself in that position. This was very important in that it has given me compassion for the people I work with now as producer.

After that, I went to work for Stars and Stripes Productions, again as a gofer. It was a very subservient job. I always felt dispensable. But I enjoyed it and I learned a lot from it. I worked for $20 a day because I really wanted the job. I wanted them to be able to keep me on as long as possible. Nowadays, you can't hire people for that amount of money without feeling that you're ripping them off. Maybe young people are missing out on a lot of experience because they're too expensive these days. When I left Stars and Stripes, I was hired to work on the film "Woodstock" to build things. This came out of my work as a gofer where I was always asked to put things together. It was great—this business is not only the designs and the Oxberrys, but also the hammers and nails. In my mind, the better directors and producers really like doing everything down to the hammers and nails. Eventually, I worked with the film crews there. It was fun. I've always liked working in the film business because it's fun.

I've gotten a lot of jobs partly through my father, partly due to the fact that I was his son. But as I got more experience, I was able to call people and ask for work on my own. Then it was a matter of getting lucky.

I've worked as a prop master. I was admitted into the Union as a prop master for a while. I was giving seminars at Pratt Institute about using tools and making props. I did a lot of freelance work as a gofer and prop master. For several years, I pulled out of the film business and worked as a carpenter. But that phase ended and I went to work for a company called Multiplex, which made holograms. Here I learned a lot about optical printing—more than I had when I was a runner at an optical house. I had gotten some film experience in my past jobs, but at Multiplex, I really had to know about the physics of film and the mechanics of a camera. I had to learn how to actually do it. My position at Multiplex grew into producer/designer/director. I had a vast amount of control and responsibility. I had to deal with clients, and I found I was able to do it. I was working long hours, and after a while, I decided to leave. I went to work at a bar, starting as a waiter, but moving quickly into a management position. It was very much like a producing job. Management does tend to equal management. You're still dealing with costs, markups, and personalities of clients as well as suppliers. You have to know how to coddle and kiss and kick and scratch, which are all producer-type jobs.

This takes me up to my present job as producer. I work full time. I work late hours, putting together packages for shipping, compiling information sheets, budgets, writing letters and methodologies, cutting up film for slides. I do get involved hands-on, especially in a time bind when someone needs extra help. It's part of my job to make things run smoothly.

Again, I'll say that what I like most about being a producer is working with so many different people. And I like seeing the end product. It gives me satisfaction. Even when it looks bad, I try to evaluate what went wrong from my position so I can try to avoid it on the next job. What I dislike about my job is the politics. The producer holds trump cards—dollar trump cards—and is constantly put at a hard edge by the client to drop these trump cards. The producer is a flack-catcher. I often feel that I'm being put on the defensive. I want to be able to cooperate with the clients' needs, but I can't interfere with an ongoing production, which has been designed, budgeted, and scheduled to proceed in a certain way. It is very hard for me in those situations. A producer is forever playing a game of seduction, and I prefer not to be a geisha.

My working hours are constant. I'm always on call. New York wakes up three hours earlier than we do in Los Angeles, so I get calls at 6:00 in the morning. For me, producing is more than a job—it's a lifestyle.

In most ways, though, my job is very satisfying to me. It gratifies my ego. It absorbs my attention and energy. I am able to feel a commitment to my work. But I felt the same way when I was a carpenter. Maybe it's not the job but the personality.

Producing is not at all an uncreative job. In melding all the elements together, there is a huge amount of creation. It can't happen any other way. That's what a producer does.

jill taffet: designer/director

My function as designer/director in commercial animation is the visualization and interpretation of the advertising agency's storyboard. Sometimes I take the basic theme from the storyboard and re-design it. Other times, I stick very closely to the original board. It's a matter of thinking about what the end product is going to look like and how best to achieve that. A lot of design decisions go on after the storyboard structure is already made. Everyone has his own idea in his mind of what the spot is going to look like. I try to think through the way I'd like it to look, how to show the product nicely within the look I would like to have. For instance, on a recent job, the board came in indicating the product against a green grid. I really disliked the grid—I've done so many grids. I tried to come up with alternate solutions for the agency. I did a series of tests for them so they could understand what I was suggesting. Sometimes the clients are receptive to changing their design, sometimes they are quite set on what is in the board.

Actually, I would prefer not getting a board at all. Often, the ad agency people don't really know that much about filmmaking. They look at a lot of different demo reels and get their ideas off those reels. It's almost as if they've taken one piece off this commercial and one piece off that commercial. The storyboard is something you've already seen before, maybe even done before. I would prefer it if the agency came to me and said, "We have this product and this is what we want to communicate about it. You come up with a storyboard." It's extra work, but I don't mind doing boards because I prefer to work on spots that I like. I can get more involved in the production. But usually it doesn't work that way. Essentially, it is my job as designer/director to make the agency's concept and board work as a 30-second film.

And, of course, I have to work within the specified time schedules, budgets, and legalities that the agency comes in with. My designs have to take those things into consideration. The more time I have, the more thought I can give to finer points and extra design touches, the more I can put into the production. But a time limit is actually a nice thing. If I didn't have a deadline, I would spend forever working one thing out. It's nice to have to finish a job in a month or six weeks and then be able to see the final result.

In terms of budget, I can also be quite flexible. I do a lot of my production work myself. I don't have a large company with high overhead. I like that, because I can work within limited budgets if I'm asked to. When I'm putting together a production budget, I'm working a little as a producer. I budget for camera, for opticals, for my own materials. It's important for me to know these costs because I have to keep track of my budget. I always want to spend more money on a production, to add more artwork, more testing, to put more camera runs into it. But I'm also the one who has to tell myself, "No, you can't afford to do this now on this job." My consideration of budget becomes an important element of my design. I try to think through the spot before I ask the cameraman for a bid, so I can explain more specifically what will be involved in the shooting. I can then tell the cameraman it will be, say, twelve runs and a bipack, so he can give me a more accurate price. And then it's my responsibility to stay as closely within that price as I can.

I tend to like to do as much production work as I can myself. At the beginning, every part of the production was a major decision. Every problem was a big problem, like where to punch the paper, where to make the kodaliths, where to buy cels, where to buy film, where to get the type set. Now those things have become familiar routines. Actually, I've started hiring more freelance assistants lately to do matte cutting, inking, 3M's, so I have more time to think about the creative aspects of the commercial. When I was doing everything myself, working on a time schedule, I'd suddenly find that I had to make 50 mattes in one night. So that's what I'd spend the night doing. I couldn't sit down and think about the exposure sheets or refining the design. Now, if I have to cut 50 mattes, I'll hire someone to sit upstairs at a table and do it, so I can do the other things. I can spend more time doing color testing and experiments with different graphic possibilities. I try to hire people that I know and like. It's a comfortable atmosphere.

My studio is upstairs in my apartment. I prefer working where I live. It suits me. I don't feel like I'm going to a job. I remember hating to get up and go to work when I was working on staff in a studio. It was eight o'clock. I didn't want to get up. I didn't want to go. I felt like that was really work. This way, I don't feel so much that it's work. I like being in my studio. If I'm not working on a specific job, I'll go upstairs anyway. I'll think about an idea, or I'll do some of my own work. I'm much more productive this way.

I went to an art high school where I learned paste up and mechanicals, and studied sculpture, painting, filmmaking, and animation. Then I went to Cooper Union, where I studied painting, design, filmmaking, and animation. I spent a lot of time on graphics.

At the beginning, I was more interested in print graphics. I did a lot of logos, type designs, and posters. I started working professionally when I was in high school as an art assistant for a magazine. I also worked doing logos and book designs. I did a book of old movie posters, and I did a lot of paste ups and mechanicals.

I really liked filmmaking. I spent most of my last year at Cooper Union doing film. But my work experience and my professional portfolio were heavily graphics-oriented. The only thing I had to show as film was an independent film I'd done in school. It wasn't professional, and when I showed it around at animation studies, they didn't really see a way to use me. The first film job I got was at Diamond and Diaferia, and they hired me as a graphics designer. I guess they could relate more to my professional graphics work than to my film. I was hired to come up with storyboard ideas and logo designs. I did logos for ABC and for the Indy 500. Then, I guess they figured, "Okay, if she's interested, we could probably get her to do lots of mattes and she'd be thrilled." And I was. I was just so happy to be working on the actual film production. I couldn't think of anything better than cutting a hundred mattes. I thought that was the real film part. What I didn't understand at that time was that designing the boards was just as real and much more fun. I guess I had it backwards then. Anyway, I did that for awhile. Eventually, they let me handle a whole project myself, designing and doing the artwork. But the problem there was that no one in the art department knew how to write exposure sheets for the cameraman. I would design a logo, do the artwork, and then verbally explain to the cameraman what was supposed to happen. It was up to the cameraman to do the counts, write the sheets, do the color testing, and shoot it. It would often come out totally differently from how I wanted it. I didn't have any control because I didn't have the knowledge to write sheets. I didn't have an understanding of what the camera could do and how it did it. So in the end, it was the cameraman's decision as to what the film would look like. It never came out the way I wanted it.

It was at that time that I left and went to work at IF Studios. It was there that I really got a good understanding of the whole motion graphics production. I was working as a designer, but I was able to get involved with all aspects of the production. I learned about shooting, opticals, special effects, because it enabled me to have more control over my designs. I began to be able to think through the whole production from my initial design concept to the final film. It was the only way I could be satisfied with the results of my work.

Then I got laid off from IF. Times were slow, and they weren't doing enough business to keep us on staff, so they laid off six or seven people. It was probably the best thing that could have happened. I wasn't really happy working in a full-time studio position, but I was afraid to quit. I didn't know if I could make it as a freelance designer. Getting laid off forced me to start trying to make it work on my own, which is what I really wanted to do anyway. I was just scared.

It's worked out very well. I enjoy my work much more. I'm making much more money. And it's better for me personally. My hours are more flexible. I feel much more relaxed working independently.

There are a lot of things I want to do in the future. I hope to have the opportunity to explore different motion graphic techniques and computer animation in my designs. I look forward to strengthening my designs and having more of my own input into the graphic concepts. I'm young, and I feel like it's all ahead of me, that I'll have more and better chances to see my own design ideas come to life on film.

mark kaplan: airbrush artist/illustrator

My background is as a print illustrator, doing record covers, magazine work. Now, about half of my work is for animation. It began with mostly background illustration work. Actually, I got into it through my wife, Yvette, who is an animator. She went on an interview with Ovation Films to show them her work. They liked her work very much, and just as a throwaway, she said, "Oh, by the way, my husband is an illustrator, so if you ever have a need for that . . .". So

about six months later they called and they asked to see my portfolio, and I had a lot of portraits of jazz musicians in it. Art Petricone is an old jazz player, so he got very turned on by my work, and we became good friends. So that's how it started. I started doing a series of backgrounds for them. It worked out very well. They wanted a Disney-esque feeling in their backgrounds, and then added a flat cel animated character on top.

To be a background artist for animation, you don't have to know how to animate, but there are related points to take into consideration, such as what color the characters are going to be and what the field size is. That information is given to me by the animation director.

I had one very complicated job—a Scope commercial that I did for Ovation way back. It was a lot of camera moves on a bouncing bottle. The camera was tracking this bottle over the background. It was a bathroom background. It was a very strange shape, because, since it would be unnecessary to do the areas that weren't going to appear in the shot, it had cutouts of different sections. It was all one piece of art, but with irregular shapes. Yvette figured out the tracking of the camera, and then Howard Basis, the other owner of Ovation, figured out which areas were unnecessary. I gave them extra bleed just in case there was any doubt about it, because it was pretty inexact at that point. But it worked out well.

So as far as my animation work, I was primarily doing backgrounds for this one studio. Then what happened was—I used to work with Robert Grossman, a very popular airbrush artist who does caricatures, a lot of <u>Time</u> and <u>Newsweek</u> covers, very well known. Actually, he's gotten involved with animation and stop action recently at Ovation, so it's gone full circle. I used to assist him when I first got out of school. He gave my name to R.O. Blechman, and I started doing work with him both in print and film. The first job was very simple. It was for a New Jersey bank spot. Tissa David animated buildings in the Blechman style, moving and reacting to things flying over them. I just had to airbrush a basic background color. Everything is very minimal color-wise in the Blechman style. Again, it was a background. But then, after a while, and again at Ovation, we started getting into actually painting and airbrushing each cel, which becomes a humongous job. But it's very exciting to see what the results are, and also interesting to get to know how not to make airbrush "boil" and flicker on the cels. I've done it a few ways. The first thing I did for Image Factory was a thing where I actually airbrushed paper drawings, cut them out, and mounted them one by one on cels. That looked great, but it was a big pain. I wound up cutting a frisket for each one initially. A frisket is a cutout of an area of the image, through which you spray the airbrush like a stencil. You trace your image and cut out on the lines for each different area of color. If, for example, a hand in an image was a specific color, you'd have to cut out the area of the hand only to make the frisket for it. Then, if there were nails on the hand, you'd have to cut out those nails and spray them after you'd sprayed the hand with the same color, so the nails would have a lighter feeling. There are all kinds of tricks. But you learn them for yourself. No one can really show you.

Anyway, I wound up drawing each drawing on paper, cutting a frisket for it, airbrushing through the frisket, and then cutting out the drawing. So there was so much cutting! And that's for each frame! In that particular spot it was a leaf falling, and I think there were about 60 drawings. But that method became too time-consuming, and I came to realize that the way to do it was to ink and paint traditionally and then to airbrush on top of it, either on overlaying cels or directly on the inked and painted cels. I work in conjunction with the ink and paint department. They feed me inked and painted cels, and I start airbrushing.

Sometimes, when it's a big production and a tight deadline, I work at the animation studio, if it is equipped with compressed air. Ovation and Blechman have a setup for airbrushing, so I can work there.

One of the toughest tasks is to prevent flickering from one frame to the next. It takes skill and luck, and I guess I've developed it through experience. There's always some degree of boiling, but I've learned to hold it down to a minimum.

With Blechman, it's been exciting doing some IBM and New York Times ads. In one particular spot, he let me design the color treatment for the whole spot. We came up with some interesting solutions. I didn't know how we were going to do it. I knew the look he wanted, and again, being conscious of not wanting it to boil, I wound up using Cel Attack Pantone film on paper, with cel overlays, and airbrushing Dr. Martin's Ink on that. Blechman's whole thing is subtlety and pastel, muted colors. The way I was able to control, not so much the movement of the airbrush, but the color intensity and gradation of it, was to practically soak the cel. You can't really soak a cel, but you lay the paint on very heavily and then gradate it out to take the color away. The technique of the airbrush enables you to fade it out by mixing less paint with the air, so it comes on as a lighter spray.

Another even more complicated job I did was the Scope commercial I mentioned. Besides doing the background, there was a rotoscoped sequence. It was inked and painted first, always with a self line rather than a black line, and I had to airbrush on top of it. I did it in two overlays. I'm always careful not to mess up the inked and painted cel, so if it's possible, if they can afford the additional cel layers, I do the airbrushing on separate levels. So I cut friskets out of paper, which is a technique I learned from Bob Grossman and have used ever since. I find it much better than film/cellophane friskets. I airbrushed the skin tones in browns and reds. There were two faces and hands. Then I took that frisket off that cel, and used the same frisket on another cel level for the grays and blacks, which were the clothes, the bed sheets, and all the other elements. So there were two airbrushed cel levels over the inked and painted cel, which was all different colors. But just those two on top of it created a real diversity of tone.

The reason I used two levels instead of one was that I wanted the browns and reds for the skin and the grays for everything else. With airbrush on cel, it's very sensitive. The whole thing about airbrush is replacing friskets. It's like a jigsaw puzzle, with different pieces cut out of different friskets that you spray through. You can't put a frisket on an already airbrushed cel because it destroys the surface, and you get a million little holes. It is just awful. It's very tricky to do a whole cel with different colors because of that. You have to think out what your darkest areas are and do them first, and then work up to your lightest areas. You have to be aware of how many cel levels there are at all times, and also of how the color you put down will darken when other cel layers of type, characters, and whatever are put on top of it. It's something I've learned from experience. You have to know what to look out for. If a color model is approved with a particular feeling in the color tone, when I go to execute it and there are five cel levels, the color has to be applied differently if I want it to end up looking the same as the approved model. Eventually, it becomes experiential.

I haven't publicized myself much so far. I'm sure it wouldn't hurt, but I've been getting so much repeat business that it's been fine. I haven't felt the need to spend the money on advertising. I'm working constantly now. My biggest slow-down between jobs is about a week, and it's all repeat business. So I haven't been soliciting business. I haven't been out with a portfolio unless someone calls me to see it. But there's always the consideration of getting better-paying clients.

Mainly, my clients are producers at the animation studios. For example, I wound up working at Perpetual Motion because, a long time ago, there was a studio called Teletactics where my wife worked. I met a lot of people there, all background artists, like Linda Daurio. She's at Perpetual now, and she gave my name to Kathy Rubin, a producer there. I worked with her, then with Hal Silvermintz, and recently for Mercury Productions, who share their studio space. It just spreads out.

My budgeting policies vary depending on the

nature of the job. There's always the occasion when the client pleads poverty, you know, "It's a low budget job, we're really cutting corners, and if you do us a favor on this one, we'll make it up to you." You always have to think about those situations. But generally, I try to stay in the area of $30 to $35 an hour. I try to estimate in my head the approximate number of hours, although often it's not right. Last night I thought I'd finish at midnight. I ended up finishing at 5:30 in the morning. Occasionally I do go under my estimated time. The more I work, the faster I get. I do the best I can, look at a job, evaluate how complicated it is, estimate my hours, and hope for the best.

I started out just wanting to do print work, and doing fine at it. I fell into animation work through Yvette, and it's been great. I enjoy it equally. The only thing is, as in all animation work, you work like crazy on something for endless amounts of time, and it's over in a second on the screen. Especially with airbrushing cel by cel. I spent two and a half months airbrushing the 30-second Scope commercial. Just ridiculous! That was a job that I really underestimated. I got killed on that job, but I hope I'll continue to make up for it on the next ones.

stan smith: animation director

My name is Stanley Smith. I'm a poor man who made it. I came to this job some 24 or 25 years ago, I guess, because I was getting squeezed out of some of the other jobs I had been holding as a teacher of art during the McCarthy period. I had some good friends who told me about a temporary job on an old CBS show called "Adventure." It was a half-hour animation show of a story by Walter Van Tilbert Clark, who did "The Oxbow Incident." It was the story of Hook the Hawk, and the director of it was a very wonderful man named Abe Liss. The producer was Jac Venza, who is now a big wheel at Channel 13. There was a painter named Hazzard Durfee and myself. I was the one who did all the running around and the menial work. We were the whole staff responsible for putting this thing together. Part of my job was running a Xerox machine. It was the first one that was used in the business. Later on, Walt Disney and other studios got them and put pegs on them. Well, anyway, this job was temporary and lasted six weeks. On the basis of the close association of these people, Abe got me a job at UPA, an animation studio here in the city. He called them up and said, "Can you use this person?" meaning me. Don, who was in charge of the place at this time, said, "Well, maybe we can." And sure enough, they did. So I went to work there as a checker—well, not as a checker—it was called an assistant director. You're like a stooge of one of the animation directors. There were two of them there at the time, Jack Goodford and Chris Ishii. But part of the job was to check out the animation, that is, you go through all of the animation drawings, and check them against the sheets. That's where I learned a little bit about animation.

The checker exists now only in the large studios. In the small places, some people don't even bother to check anymore. The last check is the cameraman, but you've got to have a cameraman who will project a little bit, one who knows a little bit about what's happening. Otherwise, the guys will just shoot what you put down on the sheets. They just shoot it, the hell with it, you know! Cameramen are just like everyone else, although it's a mechanical job. They're all different. Some do it, some don't. Some cameramen, I'm sure, temperamentally, shouldn't be cameramen at all. They should be violinists, maybe.

Anyhow, I worked over there at UPA for about a year and a half doing this kind of work and I loved it over there. It was a great bunch of people to work with. It was like being home. We had studio parties that were just wonderful— wonderful people dancing on tables and letting their hair down. Everything was okay, but it turned out that Abe, in the meantime, had started his own studio, and that UPA was falling on bad times. They started a studio in London, and they had a studio on the West Coast, which was doing all the fun jobs. They had the "Gerald McBoing-Boing" show, "Mr. Magoo," and all that. We were doing the commercials in New

York and paying for everything. Well, the London studio didn't work at all, and the "McBoing-Boing" show met with rather indifferent response. The thing was going down, and I knew it was going down, so I called Abe up and I asked him if I could come and work for him. He said, "Sure," so I did.

At that time, Abe was the creative guy, Sam was the business guy, Mae took care of the books, Pablo Ferro was an animator, Fred McGubgub was the assistant. There was a designer named Harry Duncan, who went down to Philadelphia. I don't know what happened to him. He just disappeared. And me, I was doing whatever else there was to be done. At the moment, I can't even remember what it was, really. But I must have been doing something. I was a very eclectic chap. And those were good days! We did the NBC Peacock. That was the first great studio job in the place.

Well, I stayed with UPA for about 15 years. It went through a lot of changes. Abe died, he was in bad shape. He tried to push a car with a flat tire. His heart couldn't take it. That took care of him. Too bad; he was a really great loss. He was a really wonderful person. People came, people went. Eventually, the studio got to be one of these big monster kind of places, you know, forty, fifty people. Terrible thing to happen to a studio in a city. Too many ups and downs. Overhead's too high. You can't carry these people. Business isn't steady. Can't support it. It has happened to so many studios. It happened to UPA. It happened to Elektra. They went under when they had a couple of hundred thousand dollars worth of business in the place.

At that time, I'd quit them. But I continued to do work for them. I had this subcontract from them for about 10 educational pictures. It was a big one! It was lots and lots of work. It involved driving all around the country, you know, choosing locations. It was for a social studies series. It involved shooting desert locations, Alpine locations, all of these topographical settings. That was fun in the van, the Grand Canyon, you know. Standing on the edge of the Grand Canyon, a bird flew out over the Canyon, one little bird. I swear, he just went, "Peep." And the thing really got to me—this contrast. I just collapsed on the ground. I don't know whether you can get that or not. It was a very strong feeling.

Well, anyhow, I did that. I should mention, I guess, what had been happening all that time at Elektra. I'd been working on spots. I hadn't been doing much animation. I did a project with Abe called "Genesis," which was camera moves on paintings, that won some awards at film showings in Europe. Then I got started doing TV spots, but I never cared too much for that, really. At one point, I was working on a spot for some people from Doyle, Dane, Bernbach Advertising. We were screening the film and discussing what to do about it. There were three of them, and they were going back and forth, back and forth, round and round the Moviola, and I just kind of flipped out. I started running the Moviola backward and forward and walking around the editing room. I remember them standing there and looking at me. I was directing at that time. They decided to take me off television spots. They put me on the longer pictures. That was more fun. The clients weren't so demanding. Most of them had less experience with film, so they'd give you a lot more freedom. The pictures were pretty interesting. There was a lot of fooling around in them; you didn't know whether the thing was going to work or not. There was not really too much in the way of developing this high-polished veneer that people required on television spots. It's like polishing a doorknob for eight or nine hours on end. When you get through, what have you got? You've got a polished doorknob.

So, as I said, it was a lot more fun, really. We got into doing things. The studio had the reputation of being a very hot kind of place, a lot of creative things were going on there. This is true. The stuff that came out of there now looks old hat, as well it should. I mean, that's 20 years ago now. Why shouldn't it look old? But, in those days, it looked pretty good, you know, people were trying stuff. You got good people to work on sound tracks. Dizzy Gillespie did one, Jerry Mulligan did a few of them.

The animation that came out of UPA was primarily these Bert and Harry Piels commercials with Bob and Ray. They had about six or seven animators working on these, all of them different. Their sheets all looked different. It was like fingerprints. You might think, "What can an animation sheet tell you about a person?" It can tell you a lot. Same thing with Elektra. The same guys who were over at UPA, many of them were over at Elektra too. Some of them weren't. Some of them were already old guys by then. Grim Natwick was one of those people. Lou Garmer, another very good animator, decided he'd had enough of studio lights, so he just went out to Crane's and he still works out of there. Jack Schnerk came over; he's dead now. Bard Wiggenhorn decided he wanted to move upstate. Al Euguster came in and out of the place. Terr Terricone is up in Westchester now. And so on, it just goes on and on like that.

I knew a lot about production. At one time, I was head of ink and paint at Elektra, and then I was production manager there. I was a bust at that. I could never remember anything. I had to write everything down. So I had sheaves of paper. People remember me in those days. I wore a tie and really tried. My hair was all cut and really slicked up. Pockets full of papers and stuff to remember. But I did learn a lot.

Then I did more direction. I started editing my own stuff, mostly because it was so hard to get editors from commercial jobs on the longer projects I was working on. We had a client who was the art director for Eastman Chemical. We did an industrial with him that I worked on. He was also the head of the Art Directors' Club in New York, and he wanted a film to open their club. I got the job to do that. There was very little money to do it with, so I ended up doing most of the production work myself.

Then I started working as a character animator for Lee Savage on a series of Sesame Street spots. I'd been doing effects animation and title work for a long time, so I understood sheets and I had some basic notion about timing. But I'd never really tried to move characters and give them some aspect of being. I more or less taught

96

myself how to do it, but I have to give credit to a lot of other people. It just didn't happen in a vacuum. And I don't even know whether I'd give myself too much credit as an animator, anyhow, when I think about the great animators. Grim Natwick was a great animator, and I have to give some credit to Pablo Ferro, too. He developed a system of animation. He could do a minute spot overnight if he had to, using this system. I still use it myself. You design the characters in such a way that when they look one way, they have pretty much the same shape and size as when they look the other way. So it's very easy to in-between a character's head. The same thing is true with their bodies. You work with tracing paper. It's a short cut, that's the thing. It's a way to turn out lots of animation in a short time if you have to.

The role of the animator is defined differently depending on whether it's a bigger or a smaller studio. In a big studio, you have directors and designers. The designers usually lay out their own pictures. They give their layouts to the animator, who usually questions a lot of them, throws out some of them, and works them over. Most designers don't really know how to lay out for animation. It would help if they had done some animation before. For example, when laying out a character in a field, they very often won't make the field big enough for the character to move around. That's a common thing. Sometimes the designer doesn't even lay the character out. Designers I work with in New York will do only very rudimentary layouts. That's what freelance animators get. In a sense, the animators are laying out the picture. And often, the animators aren't given enough drawings to develop a character. You have to develop that character yourself. You may be given only one or two layouts for a scene. Then you have to go by the storyboard. Let's say the character is going to walk in, take off his clothes, and do something obscene. They'll give you one layout. Then you have to figure out how he walks, how he takes off his clothes, what he does, and how he does it, as well as who he is.

In the big studios, the designer used to give the

animator model sheets. They'd draw the character in all aspects. They'd show you what the character looked like from the back, from the front, and how the character walked. I don't get that now from designer/directors. In a sense, the job of animating has much more creativity involved now. Of course, I work with the designers closely as I evolve the layouts. It helps to have a good relationship with them, if you've worked with them before, because they know how you work. But if there are significant changes, you've got to call them up and tell them, "You've got to open the track up here; there's no time to do such and such a thing; wouldn't it be better if we made a cut at such and such a place?"

I enjoy working now as a total filmmaker. I'll take the film all the way from beginning to end. I've learned how to do each stage myself. It's just more fun, it seems to me, to do the whole thing. I'd rather do even the inking and painting than hire other people to do it. The problem is that it's lonely. I remember the socialization at those big studios was really great—wonderful people, friends. Just having all those warm bodies around breathing the same air was a lot of fun. Now I miss that a lot. But this way of working has its compensations, too. It's like a cottage industry. It has real tax advantages. You can deduct part of the rent and all of the comforts. You can listen to whatever you want to on the radio, and get up and make a cup of tea.

Sometimes I have to hire an assistant. Once we had 10 minutes of animation to do in 10 weeks. There were three characters and lip sync. So I got an assistant that I had worked with on that CBS show, and we set up another drawing table right next to mine. He just followed me up on the whole thing. It worked out very well. I'd get up and make him lunch and supper every day.

The more work I get, the better I like it. I really like to work. To get a film, to work within a budget, always makes me feel like I'm accomplishing something. I've had a lot of experience working for budget. Usually I can hit a budget within a couple of hundred bucks. That's pretty good! In a big studio, they'll figure out the cost and then double it, and then they'll spend all the money. I take pride in being able to produce a job within a given budget. That's because I deal in things I know about. I'm doing almost the whole thing. I do the animation, the inking, the editing, so there really isn't that much to figure. And the bigger the piece of film, the better I do.

Most of the people in my position are not working on commercial things, as I do, but on their own films. They're working more as artists. In a way, you could say that I'm a very small studio. One job seems to lead to another, and it goes on. I like working this way. I've worked in the animation business in a lot of different positions, but this is the one that I've really stuck with. This is the one I prefer.

candy kugel: animator

I work as an animator in an animation studio. Usually, I work on 30 minute television specials, but I also work on commercials. My work begins once the film has been storyboarded, the characters have been designed, and the layouts have been made. My job is to get the actors to act, and to do it as convincingly as possible. The characters get to do more acting in the longer pictures than in television commercials. In commercials, you're selling a product, and you have to get the characters on and off and the job out as quickly as possible. On a longer film, there's not such a tight deadline. If a scene takes two weeks to do, it takes two weeks to do. If you have five characters, all emoting in a scene, it's nice to have the time to consider how they are interreacting and how they would behave given the lines they are speaking. And the sound track is usually pretty good. I like animating to the songs, because the characters get to sing and dance.

Layouts for commercials are very tight. The client has seen and approved them. The animation has to follow the layouts very closely. And animation in commercials tends to be very two-dimensional. For me, animating on the longer pictures is much more exciting. The layouts are much looser. There may be a layout for every five, six, or seven feet instead of every two or three feet. There's much more room to get involved with the characters you're animating.

We've done five "Berenstain Bears" specials at Perpetual Motion. The spots are written by Stan Berenstain, who also writes the books. He then meets with the producer and director, and they come up with a thumbnail storyboard, which is roughly timed out scene by scene. Then the track is recorded, and the editor, producer, and director get together and lock it into exact timings. At that point, another tighter board is made. It's got all the scenes, and it's done very cleanly. From that, blowups are made to the proper fields for the layouts. In commercials, the layouts are very much expanded from the storyboard. In the specials, the layouts are basically the storyboard in a larger form. Then, the animators take it from there. There are five of us, and we all work together. We know these characters pretty well by now. Some of us work better with one character than the others. When we get a sequence, there's often one character who dominates. Maybe it's Pop singing a song, or Mom or the kids doing something. Ideally, we should be working with the characters we each handle best, but we don't always have that luxury.

Our animation is still in rough form when it's finished. The assistants are responsible for cleaning up our animation drawings and matching them to the model sheets. I can always tell which animator did which scene because I know their work, but I don't think the public could tell by the time the film is finished.

The number of drawings I do for a movement depends on the nature and speed of that movement. If a character is moving very quickly and doing various kinds of wild movements, I may do a full drawing or a functional drawing for every frame. If it's a slow-paced scene, I may do every fourth or fifth drawing. I like to do my own mouths, or at least make indications for the mouths on every frame for my assistant.

The animator is very much responsible for her work. She will go over a scene with her assistant. The assistant has to answer to the animator, and redo whatever the animator doesn't accept. The in-betweener is responsible to the assistant, so as not to bother the animator. After the scene has been in-betweened, the animator either flips through it or shoots a quick pencil test to see how things are working and what changes, if any, are necessary. It works out pretty well this way.

While the director indicates rough timings, the animator writes the exposure sheets and is responsible for the frame counts. The director gets involved at the pencil test stage. He may criticize the assistant's drawing style and clean up work, but mainly he criticizes the acting and characterizations. In the "Berenstain Bears" production, the director also knows how the Berenstains want their characters to look, and it is his responsibility to make sure they look that way. It's difficult, because they're book characters. They're very two-dimensional. When we're animating them, sometimes we have to make them do things they wouldn't necessarily do. Given an optimum flow, one scene may take a couple of weeks to be fully animated.

I was an illustration major at the Rhode Island School of Design. I thought that I wanted to be another Dr. Seuss and write kids' books. But I've also always been stage-struck since I was a kid. When I was in high school, I learned that I could usher at legit theaters on Broadway and earn more than babysitting. So, at the age of 16, I started ushering and sneaking in and watching the plays. But it was never reconciled because I have the worst stage fright of any human being there is. It doesn't work; I'm just too self-conscious. Anyway, in 1970, Jack Zander was speaking at Brown University, which is just up the hill from RISD. I'm not sure what it was that Jack said at the time, but the relationship between acting and making drawings move really intrigued me. I knew that I wanted to work in animation.

So, when I returned to New York in the spring, I went from studio to studio asking for work. I really wanted to learn about animation, but 1970 was a bad year. When no one had any job openings, I said I'd work for nothing. Buzz Potamkin at Perpetual Motion picked up on it. I got 25 dollars a week for bus fare, a promise to stay out of the way, and a promise to stay all summer long. I started messengering. It was terrific! I got to see how a studio worked. Hal Silvermintz, at that point, was the designer/director. He was the creative head at Perpetual, and he had a lot of work that summer. We were doing Wall Street Journal ads as well as a couple of smaller projects. He was a little over his head with just pasting up the storyboards, so I started out doing that. It was great. He was so grateful to have someone to help that he was more than willing to give of his time. I shared an office with him. It was just wonderful! I got to see what it was that he was doing.

We were working on a Soft 'n Dry spot. One day, we had to put stick-on labels onto six or seven cans to get it to camera. I was asked if I could stay late, and I said okay. Buzz said that I'd be making overtime, and I was trying to think what overtime on 25 dollars a week would be. But I was there until three o'clock in the morning pasting down these cans. The following week they gave me a salary of 85 dollars a week, which percentage-wise was the biggest raise I ever got.

I continued working there during vacations. The year I graduated, 1973, was a very bad year for animation. A lot of studios folded. Focus closed, Star and Stripes closed, MPO closed, Elektra had already closed. I spent that year illustrating. In New York, you can always make a living as an artist, even if it's 25 dollars a drawing. But it was cheaper living then, too. Anyway, I survived, and eventually Perpetual hired me for two weeks to design a sales film. That two-week job has lasted eight and a half years.

I learned how to animate on the job. When I worked during the summers, Doug Crane was animating at Perpetual. He's a very good animator, and he showed me as much as he could.

When I went back to RISD, I started the Animation Department there. I got them their first disk, and I used their titling camera to make some little animated films. I had no teacher, but I had a lot of freedom, which was very nice. Then, in 1973, Vincent Cafarelli was hired as animator. Vinny really went out of his way to teach me. At that time, Perpetual got the contract from NBC to do "Weekend," which was two one-minute shorts a month for five years. That's why they kept me on for so long. It was so much footage in so little time. Those shows were where I really got my knowledge. Hal Silvermintz did the first few, but eventually I was designing, directing, and animating them. I also had to bring them to camera, so I got involved with what the cameramen were doing as well. It was the best training I could have gotten.

Buzz tries to keep people working as long as possible. It's tough, though. When we're working on a long film, we may have 90 people on staff. Then, between shows, when there's nothing in the house, we'll have to lay off 80 of them. Buzz tries to hire back the same people when we get in the next special. We try to be as loyal to them as they are when they're working here.

I've been kept on constantly. I think it's because I'm so versatile. I can come up with a concept, if necessary. I can board it, lay it out, and animate it. Lately I've been doing animatics. I'm not always working in the position of animator. On commercials, I often work as designer and director, and go to agency production meetings. I go to the meetings with a producer, who deals with the budget. That's a relief, because I'd rather keep my concerns in the creative area. Sometimes I'll ask the producer whether this is a tightly budgeted job, so I can adjust my thinking about the animation.

I like commercials because they're over and done with before you know it. Sometimes, though, I have a problem when the people in agencies don't really understand what animation is all about, when they try to use animation as fake live action. Animation should be total

fantasy. Commercials were different in the late 1960s and early 1970s. They were funny. They were soft-sell. And the agencies had lots of money. They'd produce eight ideas for one commercial to see what they'd look like. In the end, they'd choose one. There was a lot more waste than there is now. Also, it seemed that there were more filmmakers in the agency business, people who could read layouts, and people who weren't afraid to rely on the expertise of the animator if they didn't understand something themselves. Now, it's much tighter. There's less money and less job security. I've enjoyed working with some of the agency people, but sometimes it seems that they're on the other side, rather than working with you. Animation on commercials is a thankless job. There are always changes. I find it frustrating.

I like my job because of the diversity. I get to animate on the things that are fun to animate, and I get to design and direct on the things that are fun to design and direct. Sometimes I animate the things I design, sometimes I don't. Sometimes I direct someone else's design. Sometimes I animate, sometimes I hand the work out to be animated. It's convenient because we're all working together. It makes for a lot of communication.

When I first started working at Perpetual, I was not a member of the union. But in a profession like this, where people have to be crazy-in-love with their work, there has to be someone out there protecting them as artists. To me, it didn't make any difference. I just wanted to be there and learn. When I started working on the "Weekend" shows, I was working 70 hours a week and not getting paid overtime. At the time, it wasn't important. I could have done the job within the 35-hour week, but I wanted to try new things. I was experimenting, I was learning. I was so involved with it that I didn't notice the time. I gave up weekends, I gave up everything. I think the union is very important. Because there is a union, there is a standard. At some point, I was bound to get a raise, and I did. I've been on the executive board of the Union for years now. I'm one of these people who gets

100

involved, and I figured if someone's going to decide my future, I'd like to have a little say in it. It's a small union, but a good one, and it takes care of its own. Let's say someone has put in two or three years in a studio, or maybe even six or seven months. Maybe he gets laid off and has to start new at someplace else. Then the union says, "Yes, you are qualified as an assistant animator. You have reached that point and those wage standards." Our wages are not excessive. It's a living wage, and we're living in a city where you can't live on 65 dollars a week.

I've always wanted to be an artist. I thought I'd work for five years and then quit and do my own work. Unfortunately, my finances don't permit that. I have done my own films, but I haven't been able to give them the same kind of attention and thought that I do in my commercial work. I can get involved with my characters and making them act. But given that I have a certain amount of craft now, I'd like to see what I could come up with on my own, if I could give it my best time and effort.

I do get gratification from my job, though. I was given the problem of designing a 10-second opening for "Great Performances," and I was given a week to solve it. The logo existed, but the client didn't know what the action should be. I decided to animate the ballerina doing a real performance. She does a pirouette, and then goes back up into an arabesque. It was very hard for me to draw at first. But in the end, it worked well. I did all the animation on the dancer, with my assistant helping to clean it up. I got a lot of satisfaction from that—the dancer was actually doing the movements exactly the way she was supposed to do them. I feel very good about that piece. It was a challenge I would never have encountered on my own.

I learned to understand movement for animation using a combination of a mirror and a metronome. One of the first things I got was a metronome. With the help of Buzz and Tissa David, I figured out what an eighth of a second sounds like, what a sixteenth of a second sounds like, what a twenty-fourth of a second

sounds like. Now I know what a foot sounds like. I have the beat in my head, so I can figure out how I'm going to have a character walk, how quickly, how slowly, how long the move should take, how long a second is, what an eighth beat looks like. Plus, you listen to the track. When you have a musical number or a dialogue, you listen to what the characters are saying, and you close your eyes and try to imagine how they're saying it. Then you act it out in front of a mirror and try to translate that into drawings. That's how you learn about motion.

It's funny, often animators are disappointed when they see their scene projected the first time. I think it has to do with the fact that there are only 24 frames in a second. When you're doing the animation and imagining what it will look like, you see the drawings in a motion that doesn't exist in real life. It's more real. It almost shines. You see the animation without the separation between the frames. But when you see the footage, you see every drawing you did, and it takes away the magic. It's not the same when I see other people's animation, but with my own work, I can't help seeing the frame lines.

Sometimes I animate on ones, sometimes on twos, and sometimes on threes. It depends on what the motion is trying to convey. Sometimes twos are smoother than ones, and sometimes threes are smoother than twos. It depends on the style and the technique of the animation.

When I first started out in animation, I couldn't understand how an animator could work in different drawing styles. I always thought I had only one style. But the more I got into it, the more I understood that drawing for animation is only a means of expressing action. Drawing is the easy part. The hard part is the timing and figuring out the movement. Whether it was the ballerina in the "Great Performances" opening, copying Ed Koren's style, copying Saxon's style, or doing all kinds of drawings unlike my own: once I understood what the character was trying to do, once I pictured the character in that three-dimensional space doing whatever he was doing, the drawing would come. I wasn't one of those kids who used to copy cartoon characters all the time. But now I can draw anything. There's nothing I can't copy. When I animated Ed Koren's drawings, he was shocked to see the drawings I did. He had done four sketches for that 30-second spot, and I brought expanded layouts from that, about 20 drawings. He couldn't believe it. He said, "Who did these drawings? Did you do them or did I do them?" I didn't come up with the original character drawings. He did. My job was to make his characters move. This is the job of the animator. You have to have a certain facility for drawing, but the important thing is being able to conceive the movement in three dimensions and translate it into animation. That's what I do.

j.j. sedelmaier: assistant animator/former in-betweener

My job as assistant animator, in terms of the union contract, involves clean-up of the animator's roughs, making them consistent with what the producer and client expect stylistically. The animator will sketch key drawings one, six, ten, and so on. Once he goes over them with the designer and the producer, I get them and, working with the exposure sheets and the charts on the sides of the roughs, I clean up the drawings and make them presentable for either Xerox or inking. The Xerox machine reproduces my drawings onto cels, duplicating the line quality exactly. Sometimes there may be minimal stretch or distortion but nothing noticeable enough to affect the final animation. If the drawings go to an inker, the line quality will change slightly, depending on his own drawing techniques.

When I'm working with an in-betweener, I will do intermediate breakdowns between the animator's roughs. For instance, the animator may give me rough drawings for one, six, ten, and so on. I clean up those drawings, and then do three and seven as well, which are in-betweens. I give all these drawings to the in-betweener. It is his job to do all the in-between drawings, maintaining the style and line quality of my drawings. The extra personality of gesture, such as squash and stretch, or exaggerated movements, is usually done in the animator and assistant animator stages.

Many years ago, an assistant animator was quite different. Now, you can essentially call an assistant animator a clean-up artist, which is too bad. It used to be that each animator worked with his own assistant, so the assistant became very familiar with the animator's style and methods of working. The assistant could get to know just what the animator wanted. After a while, the style would become distinctive. They'd be working as a pair.

Since I've been in the business, I've tried to work closely with the animator as much as possible, even when I was an in-betweener, getting drawings from the assistant. The further it gets from the animator, the further it can get from where it originated. It's like the story going around the room. By the time it gets to the end, it can be very different.

Let's take an example. There's a character with a hat on, and he's going to take the hat off. The animator wants the hat to remain on the back of the head a little while after the character has started to take it off. Then, after he gets the hat off, it springs forward. The assistant will get the roughs and clean them up. But maybe he won't pick up on the chart on the side of the drawing that the movement should not be at an even rate of speed. The in-betweener gets the drawings and maybe doesn't ask any questions. So the end result will be an even in-between, with no "oomph" to it. There's no extra personality in it. The more closely the assistant works with the animator, the more likely the animator will get the kind of movements he wants.

Working in a commercial house and working in a feature studio are a little different. In a feature studio, you don't have the time and money limitations that you do in commercials. I've talked to animators working on commercials who don't even have the time to check the assistants' understanding of their roughs. Time and money are important considerations in these things. It may not be worth it for the animator in a particular job.

Here, the animator works on a freelance basis, so he's on the premises only when he brings the job in for production, or when he's screening rushes. We can always call him, but it's nice to be able to hop into the next room and work out a problem with the animator. That's the best way to learn.

The assistant should be able to read exposure sheets, which are what the cameraman uses when he's filming the drawings. Exposure sheets come from the animator and the editor. The editor works with the sound track, which is done first. He analyzes it on bar sheets, which are broken down into single frames. The animator uses these bar sheets to determine the timing of his animation. Then he indicates his instructions frame by frame to the cameraman on exposure sheets. These exposure sheets tell the cameraman what artwork to shoot on every frame, when to change the artwork, when to move the camera, and so on. The assistant should be able to understand all that so that he can check through all the levels of artwork before they go to the in-betweener. Or if you're called upon to do your own in-betweening, which is sometimes the case, you'll know what to do.

In the union studios, you work your way up through the ranks, starting with painter, inker, in-betweener, assistant animator, animator I, animator II, and full-fledged animator. So by the time you're an assistant, in-betweening is like second nature.

I was hired as an in-betweener. I was very happy to have a job and to be working in a studio where production was rolling and a dynamo was going on. Two films were in production, and everyone was running around. I wanted to do what I was supposed to do and to soak up as much as I could of what was around me. I didn't

find in-betweening difficult. But I realized that as an in-betweener, you don't simply perform the definition and draw the in-betweens, because it would be "blah." Rather, you try working with the animator at that stage, especially when you're new. You try to put in something extra, like a drag on a move, for instance. But you have to learn when to do it, when not to do it, where it's too much, where it should have been. For me, those are the things that make the difference between my first day on the job and three months later. And I made sure that whenever rushes were being screened, I was watching.

As an in-betweener, you can easily be doing every other drawing, and usually no more than three consecutive drawings. If there are three, they're usually evenly spaced. As an assistant, you may get drawings one and ten, accompanied by a chart of instructors from the animator. Maybe they're all evenly spaced and there's no middle drawing. That's when you get to play, and that's when it's fun. Unless you've got something like a building coming down and you've got to do every little brick in each frame. . . .

I've always liked to draw. I went to art school to refine my drawing. I used to draw from comic books, and I came to New York to try to work at DC Comics or Marvel. But when I saw the way comic book production was done, I found it boring. So I took my portfolio around. Someone at Channel 13 gave me a list of names of people to get in touch with. Through him, I met an independent animator who took a liking to my style and gave me a job doing assistant and in-betweening work. Then, I heard that Perpetual Motion was hiring. I took their test, and they hired me as an in-betweener.

The comic books I've done have really helped me because I learned anatomy inside out. So I can recognize easily when something doesn't look right. Of course, you can make anything happen in animation. I can change your face into a lamp. But if something that's supposed to look right doesn't, I know it. And I can fix it. Maybe if I didn't have my background in drawing, I would be able to see that something was wrong, but I wouldn't know how to fix it. I'd just let it go on through. It's been useful in that respect.

I always try to be where something is going on. If something is happening in the editing room, I try to be there. It's not that I'm nosy. I just have a lot of questions. It's a small place here. It's like family. It's nice.

Officially, if you're hired as a first apprentice in-betweener, you get a raise every three months according to union standards. Then, you hit journeyman, the top of your scale. Then it's up to the boss whether you're qualified to be promoted to assistant. I moved up really quickly. I started assisting after working for 10 months as an in-betweener. That's not the norm. But I knew I was ready to take the test to become an assistant. On the other hand, I've been working with people who've been in-betweeners as long as I've known them and much longer than that. I also have known assistants who've been assistants that long. Eventually, I want to go on and become an animator. In order to do that, you have to do your own work. It's important to have a lot of drive and enthusiasm. You have to show people that you can do it. If you wait around to be promoted, it'll take a lot longer. I play with my own ideas. At this point I'm not ready to become an animator. I can solve some problems now, but I'd like to be able to work with an animator for a while, to be able to sit down and ask a lot of questions.

My biggest frustration in my job is the time limitation. There's always a point where you say, "I wish I had more time. If we had one more day, we could do it better." As long as that doesn't become a rationalization, you're okay. I'd rather be frustrated than excuse everything by saying we didn't have enough time.

Artistically, in the realm of animation, you can basically do whatever you want to do. If I have an idea, and I think like an animator, I can express anything I want to express. That's what I'm looking forward to as an animator.

iris beckerman: planner/clean-up/inker/ painter/checker

I work in a unique situation with my husband, Howard, in a studio that is usually made up of just the two of us. We do a lot of cel animation there. My job is the handling of the production once it leaves the animation stage and before it goes to camera. So actually, my job description covers a number of different areas, each of which, in a large studio, would be handled by a different person.

Let me describe the functions as they are in the large animation studios. The work goes from storyboard stage into layout. From there, it goes to the animator, who does rough key drawings that are accurate as far as action and character. The assistant animator does the key in-between stages of the animation. Then the in-betweener cleans up the drawings and fills in the rest of the in-betweens. Next, the work goes to the planner, then to the ink and paint department, and finally to the checker, who checks through everything before it goes to camera.

The planner gets the rough animation drawings, fully in-betweened, from the animator. He also gets the exposure sheets at this time, which explain the action frame by frame and cel layer by cel layer. The planner has to check the animation drawings against the exposure sheets to ensure that everything the sheets say is going to happen is really going to happen under the camera. He has to make sure that the animation works, that the drawings are in order, that the various cel levels correspond to the sheets, that there isn't, say, an arm which is going to go behind something it is supposed to go in front of. The planner will then make notations on the drawings indicating cel levels and color tone. Animation cels are not transparent. They have a slight grayish cast, so each cel will darken the cel below it. When you're working with levels, and the color of the arm on one level has to match the color of the body on another level, you have to compensate for the difference in levels when you paint. In opaquing, generally the lowest level has the lightest color. Each cel level above it will darken it a little bit, so each succeeding level has to be one shade darker in order to match it. It's very important that this be marked accurately by the planner. He understands the level breakdowns from the exposure sheets, which he then must check against the drawings.

In our studio, sometimes we don't have enough time for the planning stage. Since there's usually only the two of us, we end up doing everything at the same time. If the exposure sheets aren't ready when the drawings are done, sometimes I'll start the ink and paint process before the animation has been checked. I'll do this to save time. Sometimes I'm better off discarding or re-doing something that was wrong once I get the sheets from Howard.

But ideally, everything should be checked against the sheets beforehand and notated for level and color. I put each marked scene in a folder once it's planned and checked. I do it for myself if I'm the one who's going to ink and paint. When we bring in other people to help us, it's essential that the drawings are checked and marked, and that the model sheets be made out for everyone who's working on the job.

Once the planning is done, the inking starts. Inking is the tracing of the animation drawings onto cels with ink. The inker relies on the planner's notations to know which level what action is to go on. Nowadays, inking is often replaced by the Xeroxing of the drawings onto cels.

My definition of inking is using the pen to do anything necessary to the drawings before the paint goes on. If we're working with cutouts, cutting out is part of this stage. It depends on the technique. Usually, though, inking refers to inked lines on cels. Because Howard and I work so closely, I can clean up the drawings as I ink. Howard animates and does the in-betweens as he goes along. All the action is defined, and the character is established. But the drawings are rough. This allows him to work more quickly. The lines aren't cleaned up. They're accurate as far as motion and character, but the final inking

technique and the cleaning up of the drawings is my job. As I mentioned, in the big studios, cleaning up is done by the in-betweener, but we omit this stage in our studio.

Painting, or opaquing, is the application of paint onto the flip side of the cels once they have been inked. The paint is applied one color at a time, and the opaquer must follow the notations in order to maintain consistency of color tone throughout the cel layers. Then, the opaquer cleans up the painted cels before giving them to the checker. He polishes them and makes sure that there are no specks of paint or dust on them.

Sometimes we will apply textures with paint onto the top side of the inked and painted cels. We can use different effects to get different feelings, depending on what the client wants and what techniques we experiment with.

I do airbrush occasionally, but it's not my favorite activity. It's become something that people ask for. I took a course specifically because it's a necessary skill these days. I've used it on a few jobs. I'm not accomplished enough to do air-brushed animation cel by cel. I haven't done enough, and don't have the necessary control. Mainly, I use airbrush for background work.

The final step before the cels go to camera to be shot is the checking stage. There are so many drawings, so many actions on different levels, that checking is very important. There's such a large chance for error at every stage of the production. The checker makes sure all the cels are in order and leveled correctly. He checks to see that nothing has been left out on a cel or in a sequence, that every inked area has been opaqued. It's so easy to make mistakes or to overlook a small detail. It gets hairy when it's just Howard and I, because it's very difficult to check your own work. If you've made an error once, you'll very often make it again when you're checking. You have to try to separate yourself from your own work. It's not easy, and it takes a lot of time. Even so, there are often reshoots because there are often mistakes that are not caught.

I enjoy my work because there's a variety in what I'm doing. I'm not sure how I'd feel working in only one of these functions all the time.

Planning and checking are very nit-picking jobs. You have to have the right personality, with a great attention to detail. And you also take on the responsibility for everyone else's mistakes. I think there's a lot of pressure on you in these positions. I don't mind doing that work here, but I don't think I'd want to do it in a big studio.

Inking and painting can become very monotonous, but they can also be quite pleasant jobs. You have to like sitting in one place for long periods of time. But it can be relaxing. You can really get into your own thoughts. And it's nice when you're with other people and there's conversation going on.

Inking is a little more challenging than painting. You have to know how to draw in order to give the lines some life. It is important to have had some training in drawing.

Painting is something really anyone can learn to do. You do have to be conscious of what you're working on. But if you're on one level and all your colors are set to go, you can really take off into your own head.

I like working with my hands, but I wouldn't want to be working only in ink and paint. I'm glad to be involved in other aspects of the production as well.

In the big studios in the old days, it was almost exclusively women who worked in ink and paint. That's where you started if you wanted to work in the animation business. And you really had to have initiative to move out of ink and paint. It's still true to some extent now, but I think it's a little less rigid. And in the smaller studios, like this one, there's so much more of an overlapping of function.

The only thing I've never felt I had to do is animate. Some animators really have that need. I've picked up a lot of the basics of animation, and I draw well. But I don't take the same

pleasure out of animating that some people do. In fact, it always surprises me that some animators who have been animating for years don't even know what goes on throughout the rest of the production. Some do, but others are really isolated in what they're doing with the animation.

I started out as a fashion illustrator, but I never really enjoyed it because I didn't like the people in the field. After I had children, I worked on a few freelance jobs in fashion. When Howard stopped working for other studios and started his own, it wasn't hard for me to re-apply my art skills to animation. We've been working together ever since.

Howard and I wanted to make art films, but we also wanted to have a family and a certain lifestyle that people aspired to in the 1950s. So our thinking went in one direction, that is, of the films we intended to make and believed in. But our work went in a more commercial direction, because we had to earn our living.

We prefer working on educational films over commercials, although we do commercials as well. We try to feel that we're working toward something, that it's a creative project. The actual work may be the same, whether it be educational or commercial. It's only in my consciousness, in my sense of what I'm working on, that I feel the difference.

I enjoy animation, and I also enjoy specifically the situation Howard and I have set up for ourselves. For us, animation is one of the last cottage industries. Maybe that's why I like it.

john rowholt: cameraman

With our camera, we shoot from flat artwork onto film. We do whatever camera and table moves are required by the clients to create graphic or optical film effects. The work comes either from animation production companies, advertising agencies, or editors.

When it's cel animation from an animation

studio, it usually comes with exposure sheets that tell us when to change the cels, when to move the camera or table, when to dissolve, and when to move a cutout. Our discretion is how to do the move, whether it's a smooth move or an abrupt move. The exposure sheets tell you to zoom from point A to point B, but we have to decide on the kind of move and then plot it out mathematically.

When we shoot for an editor, we shoot one of two ways. Sometimes we shoot to counts for opticals. The editor makes up a dummy work-print, or he'll read the track and give us frame counts. We'll do our moves and effects to these counts. Sometimes we'll shoot it wild (we'll overshoot each scene). Then the editor will edit it down for the final cut.

Most of the artwork is supplied to us, although from time to time we do make titles and mattes, and sometimes we cut out and position the artwork for shooting. We don't do it ourselves. We work with an outside company to do this, but it's been an ongoing relationship.

When we're shooting a graphics job, most of the design work is left to us. We'll get a stack of photos and pictures that we'll study. Then we determine the camera moves. We decide ourselves whether we should zoom in, zoom out, or pan. Sometimes a client who's worked with me often over the years will just tell me to do my usual thing. This is where we're able to get more into the artistic potential of the camera.

We're basically a camera service, but we also do a form of production. A camera service wouldn't be able to take artwork and compose it to shoot. We would only shoot it. If we were just a camera service, you'd have to give us complete instructions as to what to do with the artwork. We're one step over that. We make some of those creative decisions.

When we're shooting something that's going to go into opticals, it's a whole different approach. We always have to think ahead to the optical stage. Because most of us here have an optical

background, we're able to do this quite easily. When you're shooting for finished product on the stand, you have to build in all your dissolves and fades, the mattes have to fit exactly, and the titles have to be the proper size for the art-work so they can be burned in. If you're going into opticals, you can shoot all the elements separately and combine them in the optical. Clients often rely on our experience and advice as to whether to shoot a job bipacked in the camera, or to go to a final optical combination.

A bipack is the same thing as an optical, only it's done in the camera on the stand itself. The advantages to bipacking are that you get much better color and quality because it's first genera-tion. If you go to opticals, the final is several generations away from the original. When you shoot the job in the camera, you shoot directly onto color negative and that's your finished product. When you shoot for opticals, you have to go first to interpositive, and then you go through a much bigger lens system to get what you want. So your final is two to three genera-tions away from the stand.

The problem with shooting bipack in the camera is that you cannot make a mistake. Optically, you're working with separate pieces of film. It's very easy to pick up sections and re-work certain combinations. And you can see what you're fitting together. When you're shooting bipack, you're working blind. The bipack roll is in the camera running with the raw stock. You're relying on the fact that the camera is going to duplicate itself for the bipack, and that you're not going to have any problem with the two pieces of film in contact with each other. Opti-cally, the film is on one head and the raw stock is by itself. You can physically see what you're shooting.

Usually I'd say the best way to go is optically. But when there's a time element involved, or if a client is really concerned about top quality, I would recommend bipack. With bipack, you get the finished film the next day. An optical will often take three to four days. But the client has to understand going in that when you shoot bipack, there's a risk that it won't be right the first time around, and that very often it will have to be shot twice.

I get very involved with the artwork I'm shooting. About 50 percent of what we shoot is cartoon animation. I become part of it. I feel it. I know how the character moves and what it is saying. When we do graphics, it's the same thing. It's our feel that creates the look of the film. If you went to two different cameramen, you would get two different effects. You could explain it the same way and end up with two different versions. It's an artistic touch that is different in everyone. There are some cameramen that treat a move simply as a move; there are other cameramen that treat it as an art and may try to interpret the best way to move. That's how it's decided who shoots what. In cel animation, we follow sheets, so we don't really get to throw anything extra into it. But when it comes to shooting stills, there's a large amount of a cameraman's imagination involved in how it looks.

Toplit artwork is generally on art backgrounds with up to four or five levels of acetate cel overlays. For bottomlit animation, the artwork is usually transparencies or gelled kodaliths. What you can do depends on what kind of background the animation is going over. If a title or artwork is going over black, you can do practically anything with it. The quality of bottomlit artwork is much better than toplit, because you're working from direct light as opposed to reflected light. It's much richer when you shoot bottomlit.

The camera does certain effects that don't exist in the artwork. The camera makes the artwork move. The camera zooms in and out, making the artwork bigger and smaller. The table compound pans north, south, east, and west. This means you can do straight moves or diagonal moves. The compound also turns, which means you can do spin and tilt effects. Depending on how you incorporate those options, you can do any type of moves you want. You can start off slowly and build up speed. You have pegs that move, so you

can hold one piece of artwork constant and pan another piece through the scene. You can build in fades, dissolves, ripple effects, and wipes. You can do practically everything that you can do optically on the animation stand. It just takes longer.

Animation cameras are being computer-controlled more and more these days. I was reluctant to computerize my cameras because I was brought up with simple toplit cartoon animation. But the computer enables you to shoot at least five times as fast as you would without it. In graphic animation, it cuts the shooting time to about a tenth. There are also a lot of things you couldn't possibly shoot without a computer, such as curved streaks. Streaks are good effects, but very time-consuming without a computer. Let's say you're working with sixty images. You're putting sixty images into every frame you're shooting. Film runs twenty-four frames a second, so you're talking about doing several hundred passes for just one streak. You can do streaks on the optical bench, too, the same way we do them on the animation stand. But the bench has to be computerized.

We have a computer that can be engaged or disengaged from the camera. You can either shoot with it or without it. But we've found that we shoot with the computer even with cel animation. Even if it cuts only half an hour off the job, it's worth it.

On an average thirty second, toplit cartoon animation job with three levels and some camera movement, you have nine pages of exposure sheets. There are five feet to a page. You can figure roughly a half an hour to an hour for a page. So a thirty second spot could take six to nine hours of shooting time. There have been thirty second spots that have taken twenty hours. When it comes to titles and graphics, we figure about a half an hour to an hour per move. That's with the computer. It's a drastic difference from how long it used to take. With a non-computerized stand, it could take several hours to do a move that you can do in half an hour with a computer. Generally, timewise, you would be pretty safe to say that it takes an hour to shoot five feet of animation, and a half an hour to do any graphics move other than a very exotic one. Whether it's toplit or bottomlit, there are very few jobs that go through without a problem that has to be solved. No two jobs are the same, even though it sounds as though they should be. There's always something new. Maybe you have to rig up a separate system to do panning. Animators work on only two sets of pegs. They'll leave it to the cameraman to figure out how to make two things on one set of pegs move separately. We'll have to evolve a way to switch the pegs. The animator doesn't have the setup to do that in his artwork, so we'll have to build it under the camera.

Usually, our shooting works out. I'd say that 90 percent of the time we're right, because we have good rapport with our clients. They know what they want, and we're able to interpret and understand how to give it to them on film. Having that relationship helps us to be able to deliver the first time around.

We also have a close relationship with the labs. Our work takes a long time to shoot. If we get in a thirty second spot at 5:00 in the afternoon, and it takes six to nine hours to shoot, we want to be able to bring it in to be processed as soon as we're done shooting. Otherwise we'd have to wait two days to get a job out. And our clients would have to wait, too. So we go out of our way to keep a good rapport with the labs. It gives us the ability to be able to deliver one day earlier than everyone else.

I got involved in this profession the way most people I know got involved—through family and friends who were in the business. I have two brothers and a cousin in the film business. We, in turn, have passed it on the same way to our family and friends. I started about twenty years ago shooting on the stand for opticals. In those days, practically everything had to go to camera before going to the optical bench. Then I got more involved in animation and I went out on my own in 1968. For the first ten years my business was all cartoon animation. Animation was much heavier then, and there were more

studios. Then we started getting more involved in graphic animation, and I never lost touch with opticals. I still shoot a lot of art and pre-liminary for optical houses that don't have an animation stand or don't have one that's as well-equipped as mine. I shoot practically back-to-back animated specials for television, such as "The Berenstein Bears" and "Strawberry Short-cake." We're on our fifth "Bears" special now. They take three to six months to complete, and then we start on the next one. They're practically all cartoon animation, although there are some special effects. The first one was a Christmas special with a lot of star effects. But they're primarily cel animation and there's a constant flow of it. I would say, though, that now we do about 50 percent cel animation and 50 percent graphics work.

Videotape has replaced certain areas of our work, such as mattes. But it will never replace the camera. You can't get the same feeling with videotape. It's a very cold medium. It's very flat. And again, as with opticals, you're working with elements that you can't see. Opticals, yes; video may replace 90 percent of opticals, but it will never replace shooting film on an anima-tion camera, mainly because of the word "art." You're working with "art," and you can't get the same thing with tape.

I love my work as a cameraman. I've always enjoyed it because I like the feeling of creating something. I can visualize what the film is going to look like. I think that's the difference between being a cameraman who just pushes the buttons and one who enjoys what he's doing, loves the art that it is, and takes pride in what he can turn out. I know what that machine can do, and it's really beautiful stuff. I think the camera room is the best place to be. You have to use your knowledge. It's your touch that creates the film. I feel that the optical end is very mechanical and monotonous, but probably if you talked to an optical person, he'd tell you the opposite. I've been in both, and I feel that the animation camera requires much more thinking and in-centive. That's why I enjoy it. And I like seeing the artwork I'm working with. I can get very involved in the artwork for the job, and then take pleasure in seeing it on film. It also has to do with the amount of time we spend. It might take only an hour to shoot a thirty second spot on the optical bench. But it may take up to eight hours to shoot a thirty second spot on the stand. We can get more engrossed in it. We begin to feel it. Our hands are in it more. I feel that I'm more of an artist. That's why I enjoy it.

joe canestro: editor

The editor's functions vary from job to job. In animation, the track is usually recorded first. We go to the voice recording, we pick the selected takes with the producer, and we edit the takes together. If the voice track is more or less to time, we like to lock it in. We'll either open it a little or tighten it, wherever it needs it, so we're locked into the final form. Then when we do the track reading, everything is there on the sheets. Nothing will be moved around or changed later, which sometimes causes trouble. On a 30-second commercial, when you have a track that's 24 seconds, you have five or six seconds to open it up and give it breathing space if it needs it. We give the track reading to the animation director on strips, so that he can use his own discretion as to where he wants to open it up. Strips are basically the same as sheets, except that they're strips. The animation director places them down over the unwritten exposure sheets, and he cuts the strips to open up the track and pastes them down. Then when I get the sheets back from him, I see where he opened it up, and I edit the sound track to match. If he was working with sheets, and I put a pause in somewhere where he didn't need or want it, he'd have to erase all the sheets and recopy them. With strips, he can just pick up a piece and move it around to where he wants it.

In any case, we have a sound track. I do a track analysis, whether it's voice-over reading, a lip sync reading, or a music reading. We start on a squawk box. We break down each word, beginning and end. If it's lip sync, we go even further and pick up each syllable. That has to be very exact in order to make the characters seem as if they're in sync. There's really only one way of doing this, and that's the right way. People call and want tracks read, and they want it either quickly or cheaply. Well, there's no such thing. You either do it or you don't.

After we've read the track, the job is in the animator's hands. Then, about two or three weeks later, on a normal 30-second spot, we get back a pencil test with the sheets. We determine again whether the track has to be opened at that point. We splice out any incorrect frames where there is a camera mistake. We put standard academy leader at the head, and then we screen it on a Moviola for the producer and the animator. At this stage, changes and adjustments may be made in the animation. Very rarely do they reshoot the pencil test. Nobody really has the time anymore to have a second pencil test as they did in the good old days.

After the changes are made, the animation goes to ink and paint, and back to camera. We get the final back and we do basically the same thing we did on the pencil test. We put leaders on it, edit out any bad frames, and screen it.

If there are sound effects involved, sometimes you can work with a pencil test. But if there are extensive changes in the pencil test, you can't do any sound effects until you get the color back. We edit the effects for the animation, and split the sounds up into various rolls where they overlap. At that point, we go to a sound mix where all these effects are mixed together at their proper levels and balance.

Then, we match the color negative to the print and hot splice the negative. We usually put the negative back into the lab for a good color-corrected print. In today's scheme of things, very rarely would one go in for composite sound prints. Rather, we finish on videotape. Recently, I have been trying to use the flying spot scan transfer system, which converts negative to videotape. Especially with animation, if you transfer from original negative, it just knocks you right off your chair. It's really beautiful. It's almost like looking at the flat art under the camera.

I think that most of my expertise comes in dealing with the sound tracks. I've had plenty of jobs where it's really been a challenge. Like reading a music track, for example, or reading three voices talking at the same time, and having a lip sync spot made out of it. You have to block out the other two voices and concentrate on one at a time.

Whether it's live action or animation, film is film. You have to do a good sound mix. The levels have to be proper and feel comfortable to you. Usually just the producer, the client, and I are at the sound mix. The director doesn't usually come. You try to come away with a track that sounds right to you. This is a matter of experience. I also think it's important to use a studio you're familiar with, so that you know what your end results are going to be. I've done a lot of jobs where I've heard one thing in the sound studio, and something different at the videotape transfer or on the 16 mm composite print. I like to go back to the same sound studio because I can judge the quality of the sound and know what I'm going to get. I've gotten good service from these people.

Opticals are another area I work in. A lot of spots are done by rotoscoping live action and using mattes to combine the animation and the live. Sometimes I edit the live action and read the track. Then, with the animation roll and the mattes, the animation is sandwiched on top of the live. For a live-action editor or someone who is unfamiliar with animation, this may be a problem. Maybe they've never dealt with mattes. They don't know that animation is shot on twos. They don't know how to look for matte lines. They are not aware of things that could go wrong. The color of the animation has to be timed separately from the live. It all has to be prepared properly for the optical combination. Again, you learn from experience. You come to know what to expect. If it's not right, you know it's not right when you see it.

I've done a lot of live and animation spots. There's an A-roll of live action. The B-roll is the animation color, usually shot on a black background. Let's say scene one and scene three have animation, and scene two doesn't. You have to indicate that by using black leader in between scenes one and three for the person who's going to lay the job out for opticals, so he'll know that there's nothing happening at that point. It has to be dead sync, and it has to be checked frame by frame against the live action to make sure that for every animation cut there is a live-action cut at the same frame. I also give the optical house a hi-con workprint of the mattes, which are shot on a separate run, and that, too, has to be checked to make sure sync is maintained.

Often, I'll have a great deal of creative input on a job. I've had 18 years of experience. I can see right away if an in-between is needed or if a title is not the right size. I did a videotaping session a few weeks ago on a Friday night. There was a mortise shot, and we were trying to decide where to put the title. The art director wasn't there at the session. I really had to direct the technician as to how I wanted to do it rather than how the art director wanted to do it. One of the comments that came out was, "Joe's the closest person to an art director we have here." The writer was there, the account executive was there, but they really don't have any experience with visualization. Here it comes again. It's the same old thing. I've seen so many titles at the end of commercials that if something doesn't seem graphically right to me, I'll say, "It's not right, it's too big, it's too small, it's not comfortable." It definitely comes through experience and not through arrogance. I voice my opinion. I'd rather be that way than just a "yes" person.

There are times when I make my feelings known only to the director, or to the person dealing directly with the film, rather than in front of clients or account people from the agencies. I let it be known to the person who has that decision at hand. I'll suggest maybe doing this instead of that. I think that's important, because people expect me to give my opinion, and I enjoy giving it. To me, it's something that I have to offer to people. Because I've worked on so many commercials through the years, I think it's an opinion worth listening to. Not all the time, but most of the time, I feel good about it. I have a basic philosophy about that. I'll offer my opinion, and without yelling about it, I'll explain why I feel that way. At that point, if the opinion is not accepted, or if the person I'm working with doesn't want to make the change, then I back off. Then I feel, "Well, I can sleep tonight, because I've tried." I've given my opinion, and if no one wants to adhere to it, it's off my conscience more or less. Then I'll just finish the spot, knowing that though it may not be what I want, it's what they want.

I also work in live-action editing. It's a totally different thing. I just finished a live-action job on which the director shot about 14,000 feet of 35 mm film for two commercials. That's an awful lot of film to go through. Maybe it was a little too much, because it was hard to locate shots and there was a lot of wasted footage. Basically, the average amount of footage shot for a 30-second live-action commercial is 3000 feet. That's 30 seconds as compared to 30 minutes, so it's a 60-to-1 shooting ratio. That's a comfortable amount of footage. Some directors shoot a lot more. When people work with 16 mm, they tend to overshoot because the stock is a little cheaper. In a 16 mm job, you'll get the equivalent of 5000 feet of film for the same 30-second commercial. They print everything—good takes, bad takes—so you're left with a lot of footage that you have to weed through.

With animation, there is no extra footage. Generally, your shooting ratio is 1-to-1, and so editing options are somewhat limited. Sometimes, if there's a mistake in the animation, you'll have to recycle some of the good footage. Or if you're short of footage at the end of a commercial, and it's a section that's shot in an animation cycle, you can just find that section, reprint it, cut it in, and it will work. A live-action editor probably wouldn't know that. You have to know what you're looking at.

These are some of the things that you learn from experience. I've seen animation being shot under the camera. I've worked with cameramen. I've worked with animators. I know basically what they're working with, so I know

what to do in a given situation when I have to come up with some kind of solution.

You might say, a piece of film is a piece of film. But if you give it to an editor who really doesn't know about different cel levels of animation, or how the animation is shot by the cameraman, he or she could be a little confused.

Pulling lifts is another task in the realm of the editor. You'll be asked to take a 30-second commercial and make a 10-second commercial out of it. So you order another print of the 30-second negative and edit it down into a 10-second spot by reusing the same footage.

I'm also doing a lot of videotape supervision these days. People are starting to combine animation and live action by chromakeying the animation character into the live on tape, rather than going to opticals. I don't think it works out as well yet. You use a process called Ultimatte, which is very expensive per hour to use. You have your live-action piece transferred to tape and your animation piece transferred to a separate tape. You have to shoot the animation character on a black background. You key all the black out, and you insert the character onto the live action. But it just doesn't look right. You always seem to get a kind of ghosting around the character that's chromakeyed in, because you're left with the thin matte line, which tends to break up on videotape because of the scanning of the lines. Agencies are experimenting with it now, but I think it's still a long way off. Opticals are still the best way to go. The advantage to chromakeying is if you have a very tight deadline, you don't have to wait four or five days for an optical. Once the animation is shot, the next day you can have a combined tape for air quality.

We work on upright 35 mm Moviolas. A lot of people work on the flatbed now. When I cut a commercial, I know which takes to use, having seen them over and over again. I use my Moviola to locate certain shots while I'm cutting. Everybody works differently. Some people actually edit right on the Moviola with a splicer on the chair right next to them. I like to work on my table when I cut. If I have to make a match cut, I find the point where I want to match on the Moviola, mark it with a grease pencil, then do my cutting right on the table with the rewinds, mainly because I think it's faster, and because it's easier to keep perfect sync. Sometimes on a Moviola, you can vary by a frame and lose sync. On the table, I can keep it perfect. The only advantage I can see to having a flatbed is that, if you're working on a longer film, or if you're screening dailies, you have the capability of going fast forward, and when you're at the end of the roll, you can go back to the head quickly to rescreen it. And the flatbed does offer a larger viewing screen. These machines cost 32,000 to 33,000 dollars, and to me, it's an expensive toy just to be able to do that. I know people who work on flatbeds, and they say that they can work just as fast, if not faster, on a Moviola. Eventually, I'll probably have to get one, just to keep up with the Joneses, but I don't see it as a great need.

I started right out of high school. My brother worked for Movielab. I got a job as a messenger at a place called Elektra, which produced a lot of well-known people in the animation business. I worked up from a messenger to a lab expediter. From lab expediter, I became an apprentice editor, then an assistant, then an editor, all in one company. This was pretty tough to do. Usually you have to move around to different companies to move up, because you get labeled where you are, like "Joe the messenger boy." I'd heard it was almost impossible to break out, but I did it. I don't regret doing it. People appreciated the way I worked and my dependability. The best thing was going into business for myself. It gave me complete freedom. When you work for someone else, you have to worry, "If I open my mouth, I may get into trouble." Being my own boss, I really don't have to worry about that. It's nice having that freedom. You can work with the people you want, and not with the ones you don't like.

I've always liked working in animation. Elektra was 90 percent animation. I used to handle anywhere from eight to 12 jobs at once. I was kept pretty busy. I worked on a tremendous number of sound effects and read thousands of tracks. And I always liked the people connected with animation. I started out learning animation editing; I enjoyed doing it then, and I enjoy doing it now. When I get a really tough track to read, it doesn't bother me. Now I have other people in the company who can do track reading work as well.

To me, it's film. Maybe cutting-wise, it's less of a challenge than live action, but it's still film. It still has to be completed. It still has to have a good sound track. When I get back an animation picture with good lip sync, I feel good about it. Sometimes I get back an animation picture and I see bad lip sync, and that bothers me. But I know it's not me, because I do it the same way every time. Sometimes the animator is in a hurry and he'll just put in any old mouth. I enjoy seeing a pencil test maybe as much as the animator does because I want to see what the animator has done with my track. To me, animation is a short subject. It's different every time. The sound is always different. The people are always new. I accept it as one of the things I know how to do well. I just take it from there.

joel hynek: optical director

The basics of opticals is the rephotography of film onto a finished negative. You can combine two separate images into one, using mattes, double exposure, or whatever. That's the basic principle behind opticals. My function here in this production company is to ensure that all the pieces that are supposed to be combined in the optical printer can be combined in the optical printer, that their size is right, that the perspective is right. If an animated model is going to be matted into a background, the perspectives have to match. Since it's going to be my problem eventually when it gets to opticals, I make sure ahead of time that it's going to work. My specialty could be called "creative opticals," that is, taking things that would often be done on an animation stand and trying to do them on the optical printer. For instance, streaks started out on the animation stand. But now with the computers that we have on the optical printer, it's really easy to do streaks in opticals. I think they can actually be done with greater ease because of the ease in varying the offset optically and in matching them to another scene of live action or animation. Generally, you pull your mattes for the streak from the existing film, whether it's animation with something happening in it that you can pull a streak from, or whether it's live action, let's say, a woman running down the street that you want to streak. Since you'll optically pull the mattes from the live action if you generate the streak optically, it will automatically line up. If you're on the animation stand, you create the artwork, and at the same time you create your streak source and streak it. It's rather hard sometimes to make a streak source for some things. For instance, if you're shooting a model and you want the leading edge of the model to streak, you have to be quite thorough about painting out the model, which you often don't want to do. In opticals, we can pull a matte on it, and by doing an offset, we can isolate the front edge of the model without ever messing around with the model itself.

To pull mattes optically, you use either the density difference in the negative or the color difference. Generally, you're going to a higher contrast medium. You do an exposure test and pick the point at which you get the separation that you need. You can increase the separation by going one or two generations further onto high-contrast stock. You end up with a good positive and negative matte. You can do the same thing with color. If there's only one thing that's red in a scene, you can easily separate it out with a red separation filter.

The most common optical is probably putting a title onto a scene. This can be accomplished by double exposing a high-contrast title onto a scene. If it's a color title, you make two passes. In the first pass, you hold back the area for the title. In the second pass, you add the color.

It's similar working with mattes. Let's say you

want to matte a bar of soap into a live action scene in a commercial. If it's not moving, an artist will cut a matte for it. He simply makes a print of it to get its opposite.

But when an artist cuts mattes frame by frame, there's always a slight jiggle, a little bit of human error, which on the big screen looks bad. So for live-action matting, we work with blue screen, where we capitalize on the color difference to pull our mattes. Sometimes it's simple, when you have, for example, a red ball on a blue background. But when you have something that's both light and dark, it gets more complicated. You can't pull a matte in one or two steps. It's a three- or four-step operation where we have to use three-color separation of red, green, and blue. Basically, we take a negative image and play it against a positive image of a different color. In this way, we end up knocking out the lights and darks for our mattes. Then we recombine everything, so we can take a person, for instance, who was shot in front of a blue screen, and put him into any scene we choose.

Other optical situations are speeding up time, slowing down time, fades, dissolves, zooms, spins, wipes, glows. We do a lot of streaks around here these days. We have some new effects, too, where we can make an elastic screen. It's a slit scan effect that is now on the bench. We can take any surface and make the screen look as if it's an elastic. You can pull it, stretch it, turn it into a tunnel. Something else you can do on an optical printer is to change the color of one thing to make it match something else. You do this using filters. We have something called a moduchrome. You input information into it in terms of additive light, that is, red, green, and blue. It manipulates the color with subtractive light. There's a microprocessor in it that figures out which filters to use.

We can vary the texture of things optically. We're doing work for Woody Allen's next film, where we're putting him into old-time footage. This is a good example of the power of opticals. We're taking a scene of an old film and adding a movie marquee. We have to pick a stock for the marquee that we think will match the contrast and texture of the old footage. And since the old background scene flickers, we have to minutely vary the exposure of the insert scene frame by frame to make it flicker, too. Then the hard part comes when we have to add Woody Allen to the scene. We shoot blue screen to pull mattes. Fortunately, it's a black and white film, so we don't have to be quite as careful pulling mattes as we would if it were color. The problem is making Woody degrade in one or two steps. We have to make him look like he's old-time footage as well. But if we reprint him many times to increase the contrast, the matte that we have made will no longer fit. This is because film shrinks a little every time you process it, and the registration deteriorates each time as well. So it's a difficult situation.

We've just solved another problem. The old footage is jiggling, so for matting in the marquee sign, which is rock solid, we have to make the background scene rock solid. That was accomplished by making a reference clip of the scene and optically lining up every frame, on a frame-by-frame basis, to that one frame. So we made a new piece of film that is steady. We may even go so far as to optically rejiggle the scene once we've inserted the marquee.

The main reason we go to opticals as opposed to bipacking on the animation stand is when there's a live-action element. It would be impossible to matte into live action on the animation stand. The other reason is the ease of editing optically, whether it's animation or live action. You don't have to cut the film frame by frame. Instead, you optically rephotograph it. This preserves your original, because you don't have to physically cut it. And you can make many variations. You can do it once, and if you want to add a few more frames to one shot, or increase a zoom in another shot, you can do it optically. Sometimes there will be two pieces of animation shot that have to match up. This can be easily done on the optical printer as well.

Often in dealing with an outside client, the optical person doesn't get involved in the production until the end. He gets film from the editor, who has bid it out for him. It's unfortunate, though, because everything has already been shot, and it's usually more of a headache for it all to work out. In the context of this company, where opticals are part of the in-house production, my involvement starts from the beginning. When the storyboard comes in, I usually start out by budgeting it. At the same time, I try to figure out how to accomplish it. Then we either shoot the live, and shoot it so that it can work, or we advise whoever is shooting it how to shoot it so it will work.

I find my role is not always confined to opticals. When I'm in a production meeting, I'll contribute ideas to the overall look of the spot. Sometimes the needs of the opticals affect and guide the design attitudes of the director, and maybe even the writer of a film, if you get involved far enough in advance. There's a film we may be working on where we will be controlling the whole look of the film. They gave us the book—the script hasn't even been written—so we have a real chance to contribute something to how the film will look. We may not even do all the work, but we'll oversee and control all of it.

My interaction with the people that I'm working with, the designers and the art department, varies depending on the person, depending on how much he or she knows about opticals. Some people know nothing and just take my word on what has to be done. Some people want an explanation of why something has to be done in a particular way. Generally my role is to suggest what would look best. It's usually the client who casts the deciding vote. Sometimes I'll get so involved in a job that I'll want to reshoot it even if the client doesn't.

My involvement varies from job to job. Sometimes I'll shoot it, especially if there's something tricky in the job that I'm aware of, such as the composition or the exact placement of the elements in the scene. I also have people who work with me. Everyone in the optical department can do almost all the jobs here, but certain people prefer to do certain things. The optical cameraman really likes to shoot. He'll fall asleep if he has to do layouts. So he does most of our shooting. There are several other people who work in layout, who like to do both layout and color balancing.

Almost every optical could be done manually, but it would take forever. Take, for example, a zoom and pan and skip frame over many frames. You could work it out mathematically, write it down, move all the dials on the bench one by one for each frame you shoot. But with the computer, it's so simple. You just type in what you want, and away it goes! The computer controls the bench. It will zoom with the desired ease in and out. At the same time it will start a fade or dissolve, or do a freeze frame, or start a pan. The really nice thing is that it can do streaks, even curved streaks, which you couldn't do manually. The advent of programmable calculators has helped a lot. It's not difficult to work out a little program to do tapers. They're just exponential progressions. You then take the paper tape over to the bench and start shooting.

Video has an impact on the optical field. We've actually shot things to be combined on video. There's a new machine called an Ultimatte. It's quite a good blue screen device. In that particular case, it was for HBO. They have streaking people flying around on a ticket. There's no way that I know of to do a streak on video. Also, we had to move the people from very large in the frame to little dots in the distance. The live action was shot against a blue screen with one given zoom. On the printer, we increased both ends of the zoom, blowing it up at the head and reducing it at the tail of the shot. Then we added blue to the whole frame. We shot streaks that matched the people over black and then made master negatives of all the elements on separate pieces of film. We sent that out to Editel, and they put it all together over different video backgrounds. It would have been prohibitively expensive to combine it all on film, because they wanted to change their backgrounds every month. So now they can use the same elements and change the backgrounds on video.

I get a little nervous sometimes when I think about video, but it doesn't really affect this business. Here we're very concerned about design

and special effects that, I think, will always be done on film. You can't double expose on video, for instance. If you want to add something on video, you have to go another generation each time. Although a video generation doesn't degrade as much as a film generation, it still does degrade a bit.

The major frustration I have with opticals is that you can't really see what you're doing while you're doing it. You don't see it until the next day when it's come back from the lab. It can be really devastating sometimes to have worked all day on something and, the next day, find out that the whole piece is no good. On the other hand, it's really satisfying to do something that's complicated and unusual and have it work out and look good.

The reason I'm here is that this company is always trying to keep up with the technology. We're planning on turning our bench into a quad printer, and upgrading the computer. That would allow us to put a video camera on the bench. Then we could combine four elements at once and see them. We wouldn't have to rely on a double exposure. The quad printer has four heads, so you can put the male and female mattes and the background and foreground in all at the same time. You could run through it with the viewer. Or you could make one pass for the video camera. We're working toward this now. You could record on video at, say, six frames a second, and play it back in real time. It's a preview device.

We're also putting a CRT in the optical system to photograph what's on the cathode ray tube, whether that image is computer-generated animation or mattes. The thing that everyone's talking about these days is a digital electronic optical printer. It converts the color signal from film or video to a digital video signal of color intensity and placement. Then, you can combine that with a second image. Frank Vanderveer worked for years on a system that could combine blue screen in one step. I don't know if he ever got it down pat. It's really very simple. It's similar to the Ultimatte, except it does it in high resolution. You put the foreground scene, which is shot against blue screen, on one head, and the background scene on the other head. The electronic processing of it would separate the blue screen right out and combine the two scenes onto a black and white high-resolution cathode ray tube. You then photograph that onto film, using three passes with red, green, and blue filters, to put the colors back. In theory, it's really a wonderful thing. Normally it takes about a week to combine blue screen elements. The advantage of this system is the speed.

I started out in electrical engineering, but I felt it was too sterile and too removed from people. So I took up photography and liked it very much. In college, I really got hooked on film. I felt that I'd never get anywhere unless I specialized. So I decided to specialize in special effects. I got my first job as an animation apprentice, but since I can't draw, that didn't go very far. My second job was in an optical house, starting out cleaning film, processing, and contact printing. It really is the kind of thing that you learn on the job by watching other people. Opticals are very technical, so a good technical background in math and physics really comes in handy.

I prefer working in opticals as part of a full production company to working in opticals in an optical house. I'm more involved in the initial concept. In an optical house, you're often just handed film to combine. And there's a lot more of the bread-and-butter work—the straight duping, blowing up of 16 mm footage to 35 mm—service work. In a production house, you're more involved with the overall production. Every now and then, you come up with an effect that is useable. Then you're really a significant part of the production.

One of the things I like about working here is that we're always trying to figure out new ways of putting elements together using old tools. Maybe we'll take old film stock, color images in negative and positive, and put them together with diffusion filters or whatever to get something really new and unique. Very often, it has no use at all. But you just keep it in the back of your head until the situation comes along when you can use it.

Unfortunately, opticals are at the end of the production line. You often don't have a lot of time to do something unless you were there in the planning stages and said, "I'm going to need two weeks for opticals. You've got to get the negative to me by this time or we'll have to extend the delivery date." When that happens, it's nice. It's about a 50/50 mix of situations where you have enough time to do it well, and situations where you don't have enough time, and end up staying late and working. It's not like being a doctor, though. You get home more regularly than that. If you're fortunate enough to be higher up on the ladder, you can have other people put in the overtime when it's necessary. But if you're ulcer-prone, I wouldn't recommend it. Everyone's anxiety about the job peaks at the optical stage. The only people who have it worse are the people in the labs who are doing a final answer print.

I've always felt that opticals were creative. Often people say, "Oh, opticals—too technical, not creative." But what they mean is that it's not conceptual. In an advertising agency, you come up with a concept. By the time it reaches opticals, the concept is there, but the evolution of how you're going to execute it is, to me, a creative process. You're interpreting someone's idea and getting that idea to work on film. Sometimes, there's no way that an optical can contribute anything. But sometimes there is, and that's the satisfying part.

jonathan elias: music composer
scott elias: music producer

Scott: We are a music production company of many different aspects. Generally, we compose sound tracks for commercials and logos, and a fair amount of our work is for animation. We take a look at the storyboards and any film that has been shot, and sit down with a client in order to describe the kind of creative ideas that we feel suit the particular problem at hand. There are many ways to attack any creative problem. We try to offer a number of different tracks to our clients. In some cases, we may feel that an orchestrated piece is the right solution. Or perhaps, a completely synthesized piece, or a piece that is only sound effects, or maybe something that's a combination of those two or three will work better. Most of the time, our music contains at least two of the three elements I mentioned, sometimes all three. We're beginning to get more involved in vocal pieces, where voice is used either as a mnemonic or as an orchestral device. We've just handled our first series of jingles, but even those have not been, strictly speaking, conventional. We've tried to do some different things with them.

So in terms of what we do in music production: We try to identify a creative problem, come up with a series of ideas, and then arrive at the technique and the specific music that best solves those problems. We ask the client to describe the image of the company that is being advertised. Let's take the example of a job we did for Apple Computers. Their image was honest and fun. The product was for home use, so they didn't want anything too sophisticated. They wanted something that people could relate to, something almost humorous, friendly, but also sophisticated. So we used a series of synthesized bells and flute-like sounds that were in a descending mode, as the Apple logo, which is a multicolored apple, visually descending. Then you see a bite being taken out of the apple. We reinforced that with the sound of a real apple bite. That's a case where our music actually shaped the visual image. The visual was always a descending apple. But in one version, the apple bite was already taken out of the apple. The fact that we had the sound of the apple bite come after the music made them change the logo so that the bite was taken out of the apple after it descended. We were working with a sense of what the picture would be. When our music came in, they decided to make the change.

We did another job for Digital Equipment Corporation. They described their image as honest, reputable, solid, sophisticated, precise, and elegant. But the stress was on honesty, warmth, and humanity. So we had to be acutely aware of doing something that was distinguishable,

identifiable, and not too complex, but at the same time something that embodied the other elements as well. So we went for a complement of live strings doing a pizzicato.

Jonathan: There are certain keys I have when I hear certain adjectives. As a musician, I think very texturally. I'm a very textural composer. That's one of the reasons why I like animation so much. When you think in terms of texture, you're very often using more than just an idea of melody or harmony, which in music has been such a given point of view for so long. By texture, I mean quality of sound, not necessarily the sound of violins playing a melody, but the sound of the violin itself. It's the pure sound, before the melody. You can incorporate a melody within a texture. You can have a melody played by a texture. It's a conceptual view.

Animation highlights texture. It's surreal. You're in an unreal realm. The type of music that we do is oriented toward this.

When I look at a project, I very often look at it as a scoring possibility, something that will highlight the visual texture. This leads us to a lot more than just realism. In live action, music tends to be melodic and harmonic. When you're looking at animation and listening to something more textural, it takes you into a whole different dimension. A different set of musical principles begins to make sense. We try to approach live action in the same way. But maybe that's because we were brought up on animation scoring.

Scott: When we started, most of our work was done for animation companies. We wanted to work with a number of different companies whose work was in styles we liked. We didn't want our work to be dominated by or limited to the style of one particular animation company. We became more keenly involved with the problems of creating music for animation, such as the importance of frame counts. In our live-action work, we find that the feeling of the track is the priority. The specifics of where things are placed, how they happen, and the sequence of events—although they're important in live action, they're much more important in animation. We found that sense of precision and that sense of marrying sound to image very intriguing.

Music tends to establish its own identity. It has its own ego. I think that when you work with animators you can't really have as strong an ego, because the sound must be integrated with the image.

Initially, we worked directly with animation houses. Eventually, as we became stronger, we didn't have to go through the animation houses. Now we get a lot of our work directly from advertising agencies. But we still like to get an idea of what the animator had in mind, what his visual perception was, what he was trying to accomplish. We always like to see film if it exists. One thing that makes us somewhat different is not just that we like to see film, but that we like to get as much background on the company, on the images, on what they're trying to express visually, orally, what their long-term expressions are, what the frequency of this particular spot is. Music is constructed differently depending on these considerations.

In animation, a number of things that we work on are more long-term projects. For instance, with the Digital Equipment job, we felt it was very important that we come up with something that was relatively simple because, oddly enough, things that are very complex tend to get dated more quickly. The first meetings that we had on that job were with the people from the agency. The first things that we talked to them about were their images of Digital—what their images were of the people, of the product—and what their account plans would be over a longer period of time. They had a very clear idea of their graphic. They had an unusually long logo. It was seven seconds long. I felt that that would be much too long for a logo, not because it was a bad design, but often what happens with a company is that they want to have a long logo, and then later, if they want to expand the rest of their commercial, there isn't enough time. I felt that it was unrealistic to think of a seven-second logo. I suggested construct-

ing a modular logo, so if they wanted to make it a five-second logo, they could cut off the beginning or the end. It turned out well, because they actually needed to use it as a five-second logo later on. They may even cut it back to four seconds. They have that option. Anyway, we knew what the graphic was at the outset.

Jonathan: The logo animation looked very clean to me. I was taken to a crisp, simple, and clean score. The idea came to me to use a percussion-oriented, yet acoustic sound, like pizzicatos, the plucking of violins. The only electronic sound I felt would be interesting was for the graphic cursor as it came on the screen.

I came to the client with a few different ideas. One of them was to use the pizzicatos. Another was to do something electronic in nature. Another was to do something with a melody that followed the lettering of the logo. They liked all of these ideas, so I did a few different versions. My favorite was interplaying the pizzicatos and an electronic cursor sound. They liked it, and that's how it came out.

In animation, there's always something to see. There are series of tests on film. In music, you really can't judge it unless you hear it, especially when it's something electronic or textural. It's ludicrous to try to describe it verbally. You come up with a whole new set of unusual adjectives that lose their meaning from one person to the next. It's really indescribable. So, in many cases, we'll record our ideas to present them to the client.

Scott: If we're doing something that's live, with a lot of instrumentation, we'll have the client here at the studio to listen to what we're going to be doing in terms of melody on the piano. We're doing a new campaign for Crisco Oil that uses five different elements. There is a series of choral pieces. There's the background with a group singing "America, America." Then there's another vocal over that saying, "Give chicken more cr-cr-crunch!" Behind that, there's a series of textures. One is a militaristic background with more drums. One is a guitar in the New Wave genre. It's very Charles Ives-ish. It was a mutual evolution. The client came to us wanting a very different-sounding commercial. So we discussed their ideas. They wanted something that sounded like a combination of Talking Heads, Phil Ochs doing "America," and "America, the Beautiful." That was a rather interesting request. We are making educated guesses in situations like this. We felt that our idea might work. When we started laying down the scratch track of "Give chicken more cr-cr-crunch," and we saw it against the picture, it was the first time we felt as if it was going to be right. But even then, it was still an educated guess. Until we went into the studio and actually laid all the tracks down, we were not 100 percent sure that it was going to work.

We did a piece for Spalding Golf Balls. There again, they came to us asking for something different. We came up with a series of creative ideas. Jonathan's recommendation was a combination of English hunt music and rock and roll rhythms. We had a lot of percussion and rock and roll drum rhythms that were played. Yet the orchestration above that was much more classical. We had three or four French horns, a full complement of strings. It was a very interesting kind of approach.

We're doing another campaign for Eastern Airlines Package Service. They liked the Spalding spot. I think that that particular approach refined with different instrumentation is going to solve their problem. But now we have a much better sense of what's going to work, having done it once already.

For the Crisco Oil job, we had come up with the idea on the basis of the storyboard. We hadn't seen any film. We tried to develop some scratch tracks for the agency so they could see that it was working. But we were giving them a little bit at a time so as not to kill the creative idea. Often, if you get people too involved, and they hear things in a rough form, the idea may be rejected before it has a chance. The idea is the most precious part of our involvement.

We probably have some of the most sophisticated equipment in-house. It's an important aid to our clients. And we have this equipment because, for us, the textural approach requires somewhat more sophisticated devices. You lay sounds down layer by layer. If we had to rent the equipment, it would be very expensive. With synthesizers, you can't have 17 sounds all at once. You put down one sound at a time, one on top of another. This layering process becomes part of the end result. The means and the end are inextricable.

The less glamorous aspect of our work is the business end, but it's quite important. I think, though, that when a person is first getting involved in this business, price should not be a very important factor. You have to put your feelings of being taken advantage of aside, and see that you are being given a real and fine opportunity. You have to look at where it can lead, without malice or bitterness. One may be a great artist, but the difference between a great artist and an undiscovered artist is only a matter of time. You have to start with a good attitude, and remember that one thing leads to another. When you work with good people, they begin to know your work. The quality of what you're doing is more important than how much money you're being paid. We still take on projects that are not the most profitable because we believe in the project. We did a job for British Airways Concorde for Foote, Cone, and Belding because the visual was so stunning. It's not totally philanthropic. Some of it is that we want our creative work exposed. Also, sometimes we want to do a job so we can have it on our sample reel. That was part of why we did the Concorde spot. Our sample reel is reviewed often in competitive situations. We want people to be excited by what they see as well as what they hear on our reel.

Our pricing is generally broken into three areas: the creative fee, the arranging fee, and the production expenses. We try to keep our creative fee relatively high, which is something we couldn't do when we first got involved in the field. We believe that people should understand that they're paying for creative expertise. Arranging is the use of live instruments, synthesizers, sound effects, vocals, and how they're laid out and layered. Our arranging fees depend on how involved the project is. If there are a lot of live instruments, the fee is higher. With the synthesizer, your arranging fees are based on what sounds you're layering. There is arranging with the synthesizer, but it's a different set of questions. The last area is production. This depends on how we're working. With the synthesizer, production fees are held to a minimum. However, production expenses for the synthesizer are not as cheap as some people might think. You have a different kind of involvement. The in-house expenses can really mount up. It takes a long time to do synthesizer scores, more time than orchestral pieces. On the other hand, with an orchestral piece, the outside expenses are higher because you have outside studio costs and more musicians. There are also tape expenses, transfers, and tape copies. It depends on the individual project.

We deal with two or three different unions. We are composers, and as composers, often you join a Performing Rights Society. Those are the only genuine residuals we receive. Residuals are based on the number of performances and where the spots are aired. You deal with either ASCAP or BMI, the same rights association for people who write TV or movie music. ASCAP is the American Society of Composers, Authors, and Publishers. BMI is Broadcast Music, Inc. There are other things that are considered residuals called "use payments." The American Federation of Musicians is what we deal with on every project that we work on. We are AFM members, both as producers, which means that we agree to hire only AFM musicians, and as musicians, which means that for every 13-week cycle we get a use fee for our work. The first cycle generally comes out of our budget. If it's paid for by the agency, the agency deducts the musician fees from the overall fee we've agreed to. Again, that fee is for the creative concept, arranging, and production. In the second cycle of use, we're paid a use payment, as are all the people on that contract. This holds for any music production, whether it's for commercials, television, or feature films. Logos can potentially be very profitable in this respect because they can be used year after year.

SAG and AFTRA cover singers and actors, so when we deal with singers, we deal with these unions. The rates are time-based. With singers in commercials, it's a two-hour minimum call. If it goes past the two hours, you pay for a four-hour session, which is twice the standard fee. With musicians, it gets complex. If they play a line once, and then they play the same line again in a different register, you have to pay them twice. Generally these payments come from the agency.

Finally, there are mark-ups. We don't take a mark-up on our production expenses on every project. On the Digital spot, we didn't take any mark-up, because we were involved with a creative concept. The creative concept was the pizzicatos. We didn't initially think that we would need 20 string players. For a short piece like that, we'd figured maybe five, six, or seven musicians. Then, when we got involved with 20 musicians, we went back to the client and asked them for additional money. We told them that we were going to put all of our intended mark-up into additional musicians and studio time. At that point we really wanted to go ahead with that idea. The client agreed, but if they hadn't, we still would have gone with as many musicians as we could possibly have afforded.

The new Eastern campaign has evolved to a full orchestral score. We hadn't bid to do this. So we asked them for whatever additional monies they could get for additional musicians. They came up with $300 dollars, which is a little bit less than four musicians. To show our good faith, we hired all four musicians, plus a fifth out of our own pockets. Sometimes it's not purely financial. It's a matter of attitude.

lee howard: special effects director

I suspect that in my concept a special effects director is a person who, given a certain set of circumstances, comes up with a mechanical, photographic, emotional way of telling a given graphic story that doesn't necessarily need any other support. A good effect is something that will stand by itself. A good effect is something that is very ordinary happening in a very unusual way. A good effect is something you should never realize happened in a film. If you can see it as an effect, then it's an academic playground. But if it is so integrated that you believe it, that is a good effect. You're never aware that it's an effect. A good effects director is someone who solves the problem of visually telling a story. Another thing I find essential in a good effects director who is designing film effects is an intimate knowledge of the camera. This is almost a third of what you can work with, and in some cases, it's half of what you can work with. I can play games in the camera that require very little if I know the camera intimately. I can achieve an effect in the camera that would otherwise require, say, eight elements for optical compositing. For example, we did a "Sure" spot where a scan of a clock was overlaid on the product shot. But rather than using separate elements, I actually re-exposed one complete piece of animation a second time with absolute precision. What was great about it was that we ended up with one original, first generation final negative. I really enjoy being able to reproduce an effect without regenerating the image through opticals. I am totally aware of the sophistication of optical systems. I've seen them operate. In many cases, opticals are the only way to achieve certain effects. But if one can go out on a limb and take a chance, which is what one does when making eight or 10 passes on negative within the camera, the end product can be so far superior. It is risky. You do have to do a lot of testing. But I don't believe a good effects person can avoid doing a lot of testing. For every foot of finished film we turn out, I'm sure we shoot 20, 30, 50, 100 feet of testing, depending on the job. Sometimes we have to shoot 500 feet to wind up with three feet of beautiful film. It's essential. Each time you test, you learn a little bit more, and you can hone an image and its components to an exact, fine state, which I think is what a good effects person should be doing.

I was asked to shoot a bag of candy that turns from horizontal to vertical as candy falls into it. We shot the candy falling out of the bag, of course, and in reverse, it would appear to be falling into the bag. In doing this, normally you would turn the camera upside down, because of the relationship of the sound track to the image on the 35 mm frame. This made me a little crazy. I spent a night thinking about it, and I came up with a system by which I can shift the image from the left to the right area of the frame. Thereby, I can shoot with the camera right side up and rotate the film, never changing the emulsion relationship, to get an upside-down image. I don't have to run the camera upside down. I simply realized that if you look at a piece of film and see where the centers are, what Academy aperture is, what full frame is, you can shift it. It's just a matter of judgment. So I made new mattes for the camera. Now I have a set of mattes with which I can shoot upside-down images without turning the camera upside down. It may seem insignificant, but it struck me that for the last 40 years, people have been turning cameras over. If you don't have to do this, you are in a much better position. Working with a camera right-side up allows you to move the camera on any geared-head tripod with great precision. When it's upside down, then you're off the nodule point, the center of the lens, so it's very difficult to pan and tilt. You're always panning and tilting in an arc.

I shot a sloppy test and it worked. Today I made the mattes, and tonight the footage of the mattes is going into the lab. Tomorrow, we'll have the new mattes to put into the camera. We'll be able to shoot with the sound track on the right or the left, at our will, without having to do any work or any more testing. That's a big step ahead. I don't know why no one else has thought about doing it. It's my understanding of the relationship of an image to a given field, to academy aperture, to full aperture, to TV cutoff. It's not difficult—it's pure geometry. This is the kind of thing that can make special effects shooting so much easier.

There are other effects that can be done within the camera by making a number of passes with the film. You can actually paint with light on frames of film. You can learn how to fog film a pale blue or a rich Ultramarine blue in a sky with stars, rather than having a black sky with stars. You can learn how to be able to predict what your film will look like. You have to be willing to take risks and make mistakes. You have to become intimate with the film.

Many times we shoot things in 4 by 5 for test work. Shooting with a 4 by 5 bellows camera is the same game as shooting with a 35 mm motion picture camera. The format is different, but the relationships are the same. Once you have the background knowledge, the exploration you can do with it is endless. The surface has barely been scratched.

I mentioned scan. Since "2001," slit scan has become very popular. The principle has been around since the nineteenth century, called streak photography. It's very much like pointing a camera at the night sky and allowing the stars to leave streaks on the film with an eight-hour exposure. That principle is not new. But using it for a graphic purpose is a very exciting thing. A good effects director took this simple information and reapplied it to come up with what is today a whole new area of graphics. I was very intrigued by it and built a scan machine. It's the kind of thing one builds and rebuilds, and plays with more and more. I think everything that I've seen in scan, including my own work, has barely scratched the surface. It has endless potential for painting with light to imply dimension on film. It's all totally abstract. While you're doing it, you don't see it. You have to imagine what the film is seeing. You present certain information before the camera. You light it in a certain way. You control what the film sees and how long it sees it. After a while, your mind starts to be able to think like the camera. You begin to know that you can control and repeat certain things. You can make certain aesthetic judgments, which is very exciting. I look forward to doing more experimentation with scan.

Scan is essentially done with a computer programmed, multiple compound, linear motion tracking system. The same equipment is used for shooting products that fly or move. It allows for great precision. You can make double and triple passes in order to pull mattes. Few people seem to do this, but you can shoot mattes at the same time that you're shooting your animation. It's done by triple framing. The first frame is the subject lit on a black field. The second frame is a backlit screen with a silhouette of the subject, which becomes the matte. And the third frame, and fourth and fifth frames if you want, are details of light shot frame by frame to highlight various parts of the subject. Then the frames are separated on an optical printer and composited. You can control how much glow you have on the subject, what color the subject is. The registration is absolutely accurate all the way through because all you've changed for each frame is the lighting. This way you don't have to make four, five, or six passes to get the desired effects. The potential for error in multiple passes is great, especially when the changes from frame to frame are very small.

The term "motion control" is very new in the industry. But we've been building motion control systems for fifteen years. It's amusing. It's not new, it's just popular now. It wasn't called motion control. We called it a linear tracking system. It's just hardware. It's important not to allow hardware to dictate what you do. Machines are great if they're doing what you want, not if you're thinking the way they are capable of working. You shouldn't bend your mind or your aesthetic judgment to the machine's capability. A lot of people do that, especially with animation stands, and it's very sad.

Being able to perceive of what animation is, and being able to think in terms of 1/24 of a second, conceptually, is a very good discipline for any form of motion pictures, whether it be live or effects. You have to be able to deal within that small fraction of time and realize what the camera is going to see. We recently had the job of peeling a real apple in 96 frames. It became an exercise in concentration, testing, learning, and becoming intimate with the act. How does an apple peel? What happens to it when you're peeling it? Where does the peel naturally curl? What apples work? What apples don't? What is the best way to view this act? How do you control the speed of the peeling? The top of the apple is smaller in diameter than the middle of the apple. So the top peels off faster than the middle because it has a smaller circle to travel. That kind of thinking can be applied to an apple, to a can, to any object, to any geometric shape. You can animate any shape. You can metamorphose it from one shape to another. You can manipulate space and time. You can make the unreal real, and not only real, but excitingly real.

We commonly work with time lapse photography. Time lapse is another form of stop motion. An intervalometer is attached to the camera. It is a timing system that dictates intervals. You can set this timer to shoot one frame every eight seconds, or whatever. Thus you can break a 10-minute baking cycle of a cookie down to six seconds of film. You can do this with anything. You've seen time-lapsed clouds, where the clouds seem to be rolling toward you. I've sat up on the roof and shot 800 feet of clouds rolling over this building in time lapse. I can leave the camera up there all day, and it will just merrily shoot a frame every 90 seconds. You are actually changing the relationship of time to the eye. Shooting time-lapsed cookies was a little more difficult. We had to control the temperature. We had to make it look beautiful. And at the same time, it had to be shot in the proper number of frames for the job. First we set up an oven to bake the cookies and determined the best lighting solution. We figured out how long a cookie takes to bake by baking the first one. It turned out that these cookies took about 11 minutes. Then by doing a simple bit of calculation, we reduced that to six seconds, or 144 frames, which meant we set the intervalometer to shoot a frame every five seconds. We shot it through 10 or 12 times, varying temperature, lighting, timing. We looked at all these tests and decided what worked better, what was lit better, what looked more appetizing. Then we did it again. In the cookie job, which was only 144 frames, we must have shot 85 to 100 cookies before we established an exact principle system for getting the perfect baking cookie. We played with lighting, loading of the oven, timing of the shooting intervals. We experimented with the cookie dough recipe, the cutting of the cookie, the placement of the chocolate chips. We built

reflectors in the oven to light the edges of the cookie inside the oven as it was baking. Three weeks later, we ended up with a beautiful cookie.

The same thing was true for another job we did involving a rose that metamorphosed from rotten and dried up to a beautiful, lush rose against a glowing, apricot-colored background. The basic technique for drying up a rose is to heat it with infra-red lamps. We had to do this and shoot it in reverse time lapse. We decided to heat the rose on a piece of Pyrex glass, but first we had to find the right kind of Pyrex. We broke many pieces of glass in the process, because when you get up to 190°, glass breaks, even Pyrex. We eventually ended up using a piece of tempered Pyrex. We backlit the rose, diffused it, and added color. It was a very beautiful, cosmetic, 7½-second shot. We shot that, too, probably 50 or 60 times until we got the right timing, lighting, and heat cycle. We had to set up a simple computer to turn on the heat lamps, bake the rose, turn off the heat lamp, shoot a frame of film, turn on the heat lamps again, and so on. But the cycle changed as it went on. For the first four minutes, it was a frame every three minutes. Then it became every 90 seconds, then every 60 seconds, all the way up to one frame every 45 seconds at the end. Once we'd figured out the timing cycle, we programmed the computer to make the changes. Then we could work with changing light, finding a better rose, adding a petal here or there. But the act of timing was handled better by the machine.

We build those kinds of machines, because in many cases, the programmers who are available don't do what we want. They aren't adaptable enough to think the way we do, and so we oftentimes have to build our own equipment. Probably one of the biggest jobs of a good effects director is being willing to discover that there is a problem in achieving an effect, and that there isn't equipment available to do it, and being able to design and build the necessary equipment. Sometimes it's frightening. It costs a lot of money, and you can be wrong. I've thrown out a lot of junk that I've built because it

124

didn't work. But I've also ended up with some pieces of equipment that don't exist anywhere, that do things that no one else can do, only because I've built and rebuilt until it worked. With the scan machine, for instance, I think I'm going into my eighth rebuild right now. But each time I do it, I've learned more, and I can give the machine more abilities. It gives me a greater reach aesthetically, intellectually, and emotionally. I have more fun with it. That's important. If it isn't fun, you shouldn't do it. If it isn't fun, you won't do a good job. If you don't do a good job, people won't want to pay you. If people don't want to pay you, you'll get depressed. And the more depressed you get, the worse your job will become. Eventually you'll do a very bad job, and nobody will want to work with you. But if you do only that which gives you fun, you'll find that you never limit the amount of fun you should have, and your product will turn out that much better for it. Personally, I find it challenging to do some of the things that clients require, whether it be a product demo, something floating in the air, a microscopic view of bubbles rising. These are rather exciting projects for me. They may end up as commercial segments of a TV spot, but the act of doing them is, for me, a form of knowledge, a form of learning, a way of exploring an area I've never been in. I don't think anything in this world can be more exciting than exploration, in land, or information, or images, or feelings. Exploration is probably the core of life. Without it, we'd all be very dull piles of salt.

I started out as a puppeteer. I'd been building puppets since I was seven years old. When I was 14, I did my first professional puppet show. After high school, I ran out and got a job at a company called Sue Hastings Marionettes, which traveled around to schools doing kids' shows, like Winnie the Pooh and Toby Tyler. For a couple of years I worked there. At one point, we got a job to shoot a puppet television series called "Betsy and the Magic Key." So for a year, I did nothing but puppeteer this film. After the series was over, I went to work for the film company and found that very exciting. At that juncture, I started my own studio. I built puppets for other people, and I also built a night club act that I

used for a few years. But I got more and more into films. I enjoyed being able to play in time and space. I think puppets are great, but in film, there seems to be so much more field for exploration in time, space, form, object, color, and motion. Film allows you to do all of that. It's like a big playpen.

The studio here is set up as a film studio. We have equipment, we have a shooting stage, we have lights, and all the other paraphernalia for motion pictures. But we also have a very elaborate shop, art department, sculpture department, and laboratory. We integrate a great many of these things so that we can create machines, models, objects, and images from any source. It may be built three dimensionally. It may be painted. We paint backgrounds when we need them. We don't go out and find them. What's unique in this studio is the ability to just do it. We have a group of people here who are really family—artisans, mechanics, animators, camera people. We have our own lab. We do our own slop tests many times so we don't have to wait for a commercial lab. We just look at the negative to make certain judgments. And I live here as well. When I bought this place, I knew that I had to live very close to where I work. I don't work nine to five. Most of my inspired work occurs outside the nine to five area. Nine to five is usually answering phones, and dealing with business problems and clients. There's really little that I can do creatively. It's from five to nine in the morning, or from six on at night, or weekends, that Bob and David, who also live in the building, and I often meet to set up and shoot things. One of us may just buzz the others on the intercom and say, "I've got a great idea! Let's try it!" In five minutes, we're all together, the camera's loaded, and we do it. It doesn't have to work. It doesn't have to be right. It just has to prove a principle, and if we find it intriguing enough, we will refine it and make it work. I would feel very hamstrung if I were in a situation where everytime I wanted to shoot something, I'd have to rent a stage, rent equipment, move lights, and then have eight hours to quickly do it. There are people working in that position. I'm very aware of how lucky we are to have the facilities here that we do have. I think most of the good creative things happen outside of that nine to five period. You can be creative during a shoot day, you can change things, make judgments. But the really exciting things happen outside that time, when you aren't pressured by answering phones, talking to people, dealing with all the aspects of business, which really consume a lot of time. Once I actually logged myself—I talked to 78 different people in one day on the telephone! It doesn't leave much time for work.

Most of our work is commercials, with occasional documentaries and television specials, and rarely, some feature work. Most of our clients are people from advertising agencies. They bring us a storyboard, which in some cases, we will execute quite accurately. In other cases, if I find something that I think will help tell the story, I will shoot a test. I do that a lot. I've discovered that shooting a test and actually showing it to someone on film has much more clarity than verbally describing an idea. In many cases, I've come up with another version of a storyboard and shot tests to show the client. Sometimes, they will actually change the storyboard because it does work better. It tells a better story. It's better theater. It plays. Basically, that's what a commercial is. It's a little piece of theater. It's a 30-second play. It has a beginning, a middle, and an end. And if it's a good commercial, it doesn't bore you because you're not even aware that it's a commercial. If it's a bad commercial, it's just dogma. I've been very happy with the fact that a number of clients have given me the opportunity to add my creative input to certain ideas. Sometimes, it will make a job really work well and become a classic little thing as opposed to a mediocre, standard commercial.

At times, I am not too accurate about costs. If I find a job very exciting, I won't even charge for the work I put in. But that's totally an emotional choice that I make. I think it's very important, especially in aesthetic areas, that you feel what you do. You don't just execute it. This cut-and-dried, let's-chop-it-out-and-get-it-done-with attitude I don't like and don't want. It doesn't happen here at the studio. There are a lot of clients in advertising agencies who call to dis-

cuss a technique of shooting something, or even a board, that I'm not even interested in bidding on. They're friends; I know them. I will often give them my own interpretation or creative input to help them. It becomes a good mutual relationship. If it's something I can do, I might very well get the job by sitting down and giving them my time and my thoughts. And whether the job is a $100,000 job or a $500 job, I think one really has to apply the same kind of concentration. I don't ever cheat that way. It's not in my makeup. I give myself totally to anything I do, whether it be big or small. Maybe my motto is, "Do the best you know how, find the best solution, and go one step further."

ephraim cohen: computer animator and programmer

I started out as a mathematician. In the mid-1960s, it became important for me to get out of school and into something that would keep me out of the army. So I started working with computers at Bell Laboratory in the anti-missile systems program. It was a large, useless military endeavor. It became operational in 1972 for one day, and then it was officially shut down. It was a real terror. After the war was over, I quit the job and did nothing for two years. When my money ran out, I started looking for jobs. At that point, all I was qualified to do was computer radar work, and I didn't enjoy any of the jobs I got. So I decided the rational approach wasn't getting me anywhere. I went to Kansas, where I'd once gone to school. There was a sculpture conference there, where I met a fellow named Ron Resch, who was a computer sculptor. He had a grant, and he needed someone to figure out a number of mathematical problems that he had. He was a professor at the University of Utah, which at that time had a very large grant from the military to do research in computer graphics. If you trace everything in computer graphics back, you find that most of it ends up at the University of Utah in the early 1970s. It's where a lot of the concepts and the basic work were done. The grant stopped in 1973. The government's excuse for stopping the money was that they decided that what they were paying for was inevitable. That is, there was no reason to pay for the development of computer graphics, because it was going to happen anyway, whether the government supported it or not.

Anyway, I ended up in Utah for a couple of years working for Ron Resch. He makes these peculiar folded sculptures. I worked mostly folding thin plastic sheets. It turns out that you can fold material in much more interesting ways than you'd normally imagine and make very attractive objects out of it. I figured out the physics of folding a sheet of paper, the way it bends when a fold is made. I made computer simulations of folding. More to the point, I created a system that allowed you to design an object in three dimensions.

If you start with a curve on a sheet, what are all the possible curves that it can be folded up into? And, of more interest, starting with a curve in space, what are all the possible curves that you can draw on a sheet that would fold up into it, and how do you fold it to get to that curve? I wrote a computer program that would allow you to specify a curve in space, as well as the kind of surface you wanted. Then the computer would draw a plan in two dimensions. Furthermore, it produced a control tape for a plotter that would actually do the scoring so we could more or less produce the finished art by machine. I also worked on another program that made pictures of what the folded surface looked like, in terms of viewpoint, color, light source, and how the surface reflects light. It's all mathematical imitation of the laws of physics.

So my involvement with computer graphics grew out of my mathematics background, my experience at Bell Lab, and my artistic background. I can draw quite well, and I paint a little.

Animation is something I never did for fun. It's always been a job. After working in Utah, I took a job in Massachusetts doing computer-aided design. It was mostly three-dimensional line drawings. And then, I went to New York Institute of Technology, where I got back into making solid-looking, three-dimensional pictures. There were quite a number of projects I worked on at NYIT. One was a two-dimensional animation program, doing conventional animation. Whatever two-dimensional animation I learned was actually computer animation. I'd draw pictures into the computer, color them on the computer, and send them out to video tape so you could instantly see them and make changes. It was a very fast education in animation for me. The first job that the Computer Graphics Lab at NYIT did was called "automatic in-betweening." That is, the animator draws two extremes and the computer calculates the in-betweens without human intervention. If you ask me, it just can't be done in many cases, because it's trying to replace the human in-betweener. There are a lot of problems like this that salespersons predict computers will be able to solve within the next five or 10 or 25 years. The one I came across first was "automatic translation," where you can feed a Russian document through the computer and it will come out in perfect English. In the 1950s, people were seriously trying to do this. But the results never worked. This is because a human being brings to a translation much more information than can be stored in the computer conveniently. There are a few old jokes, translating an English sentence into Russian and then back into English and seeing how it comes out of the computer. For example, "The spirit is willing, but the flesh is weak" comes back as "The ghost is ready, but the meat is raw." A more obvious one is "Out of sight, out of mind," which comes back as "Invisible, insane." The same kind of problems come up with automatic in-betweening. For instance, if an arm is starting off to the side and swinging forward, the computer drawings that follow that action don't really relate to each other as drawings. They relate only as three-dimensional shapes being described. The computer cannot look at a set of lines and recognize what the drawing is. People seem to do this instinctively. It's even difficult for the computer to understand what is inside and outside a set of lines. I don't consider the computer to be a successful tool in-betweener. It does prove to be useful in simple cases. If an animator designs specifically for a system like this, he can take advantage of the computer to do a lot of the in-betweens. But he must cater to the limitations of the computer.

The people who have been using this system are conventional animators, so their key drawings are done in the conventional manner. There are generally three, four, or five in-betweens, in the cases where they can use the system. In other cases, they demote themselves to in-betweening and do every drawing.

The most successful part of the program is the ink and paint system. We have more animators here than inkers and painters. In fact, there are only two and a half people doing ink and paint, one of whom does other things as well. Ink and paint is a pretty tedious job. I mentioned before that it's hard for the computer to know what's inside and outside of a group of lines. It's hard, but it is possible. Most of our ink and paint is done by having a person touch down in an area with an electronic pen. The computer colors in that area with the designated color until it hits lines. It eliminates the problem of neatness. You just touch an area and it gets filled up with color. Then you go on to the next area. It can be made even more automatic than that. Hundreds of drawings a day isn't unreasonable to ask of somebody working with the system.

Recording of this animation on tape or film is also an automatic procedure. You have a background, which has been painted with the computer paint system. And you have a number of "cels," which the computer knows are supposed to be transparent. The computer assembles a frame much the same way as a person would do under the animation camera. The computer memory device for holding a picture is called a frame buffer. First the background is put into this picture; then each of the cels, in the order that the animator has chosen, is laid over the background picture. The transparent areas allow what's already there to remain unchanged by the overlay. When all this is done, it can be seen on a TV set, and fed into a tape recorder. The tape recorder is controlled by a computer to record one frame at a time.

The person who is half an inker and painter is the one who tells the computer what goes into each frame. It's really a secretarial job. He just sits there with the animation sheets and types them into the computer.

The information on the original exposure sheets has to be translated into a language that the computer can understand. The original sheets are really for communicating with people. There is typically a great big X where there's a cross-dissolve. There's no way to type in a great big X. So you have to get the information across that the cross-dissolve starts on one frame, ends up on another, and that each scene has a different value at each frame in between. That information is an auxiliary list of commands that accompanies the rest of the information that makes up the imagery. The program combines all the information into an exposure sheet that the computer can understand. It has the full information for each frame.

You have to realize that the people involved in a computer animation production are the same as those involved in a conventional animation production. The computer is only a tool that helps them do their work. The animators animate and write out the sheets. The ink and paint people ink and paint. The computer just makes their work a lot faster and easier, but it doesn't completely handle the job. Each drawing still has to be checked by a person on the TV screen. One advantage of using the computer is that there are no animation cels, so they can't get dirty. And they are pretty easy to correct. And they're unfortunately very easy to lose. That's one of the disadvantages of not having actual cels. If something goes wrong with the storage medium, which is magnetic disks, the work is just gone, as if it never existed. There are ways of avoiding this, by making copies of everything as you go along. Basically, the structure of computer animation is carefully copied from conventional animation, partly to make the animators feel more comfortable. And it's wrong to think that we, being new to the field, could create a better system for doing animation.

I also do some design work here, such as the Lifesaver commercial we did. An advertising agency from Canada came down and looked at our sample reel. About a month later, they sent us three large drawings that were ideas for a Lifesaver ad. One of them showed a bunch of Lifesavers inside a tunnel that was supposed to be the inside of a Lifesaver pack. I thought that one had some real possibilities, so we selected that one. The ad is not all computer animation. It starts with a model of a roll of Lifesavers that opens up. Then you go flying down the tunnel. Inside the model was a blue chromakey surface that was used as a matte for the computer animation. The main reason I wanted to work on this spot was that I had ideas about changing rates of things as a way of animating. The speed going down the tunnel wasn't just accelerating. The acceleration was accelerating. It was not just going faster, but somehow going a little faster than you expected it to be going. The other thing that happened was that the Lifesavers were flying at you from down the tunnel. They were all three-dimensional computer generated pictures. We had a plaster model of a Lifesaver made and photographed. We measured the photographs and reduced the Lifesaver to a bunch of numbers, telling the inner and outer radii, how much of a bulge, how much of a lip.

Getting the lettering on was another story. Lifesavers do say "Lifesavers" on them, and ours did too. We made them look slightly transparent by the way they were brought in. As I mentioned, the pictures are assembled in the frame buffer. So, as each Lifesaver was brought over the background, rather than being brought over opaquely, that is, replacing the background, it would look at the background and become a combination of 10 percent of whatever was already there, and 90 percent of its own color. So we got transparent-looking Lifesavers, except for Peppermint, which isn't.

Different computer animators work differently. I know how to write programs, so faced with a problem, I'll start writing a program to solve it. Usually, animators aren't so good at writing programs, so faced with a problem, they figure out how to use the programs they've already got to solve it. I wrote a lot of programs for the

Lifesaver ad. Some of them weren't really necessary; they just made the work go a little bit faster. The background was generated by a special-purpose program, but I could have done most of it in other ways. Even the animation was a special-purpose program. It figured out when to start a new Lifesaver at the end of the tunnel, and on each frame, it selected which image of it to use.

Clients usually arrive with a storyboard that they want represented with animation. I usually consult with clients to try to get the boards to work as I see them. Sometimes I am able to do my own boards. That makes the work go a lot faster, because I keep the design much closer to the easy ways of doing things. Easy, that is, for me. Someone from the outside can ask for things that seem easy and really aren't. I find storyboards are a very important way of communicating ideas. A few years ago, it was really a problem. No one could draw storyboards for us, because they didn't know how to represent computer-looking imagery with little sketches. Nowadays, designers all know what computer graphics look like. They can sketch out rough boards, and even though their drawings don't look like what's going to end up on the screen, at least everyone has a pretty good idea of what to expect. That's all storyboards ever were. They weren't supposed to look like what would end up on the screen. They are just a way to communicate what someone wants.

I think computers are still fairly limited as to what they can do. If I asked whether I could animate a normal human being, a man wearing a business suit, it wouldn't take me a tenth of a second to say, "Absolutely not!!" The computer just can't handle that right now. I do want to keep qualifying everything. There are an awful lot of "computers can't do . . ." statements. I don't have enough faith to say anything like that. But I will say that computers have never done a man wearing a business suit at all convincingly. If you want a man wearing a business suit, the cheapest and most effective solution is to hire one and film him live.

What the computer does well is work with

surface treatments. There are several different computer "looks." There's two-dimensional animation, which I expect has a great future and almost no past. There are a lot of people working in it now. There's a system in Japan that inks and paints normal animation done on paper. The system scans the pencil drawings into the computer, and then the computer is used to paint them in. Then the colored images get recorded. But it's still the studio animation look. Then there's what we call three-dimensional animation. The pictures are still flat, of course. In three-dimensional animation, the computer is given information about the three-dimensional aspects of a form. So two pictures could look exactly the same, but one would be two-dimensional and one would be three-dimensional. The difference lies in what the computer knows about the picture. The easiest example is a cube. If the computer were told where all the points lie on the paper and how they're connected with lines, that would make it a two-dimensional picture. If the computer were told where the points lie in space and from what viewpoint the cube is being seen, that would make it a three-dimensional picture.

My style of working is pretty wearing. Sometimes I don't do anything for months at a time. I'll just meet with people and discuss projects, but I won't draw a picture or write a program. Then when I start working, I'll stop eating and sleeping, and work till 5:00 A.M., sleep for a few hours, and then come back. I do that until I get burned out again. I seem to have a good sense for how long something will take. If I need a hundred hours to do a job, about five days before, I'll get really charged up and start to work on it. I usually get done more or less on time.

We're looking to get into video games. I think video games are animation—at this stage, extremely bad animation. That's not an unhopeful sign. It means that there's nowhere to go but up, and up can go very far. The idea of having animation that the viewer interacts with is very exciting. If you look at a video game as a novelty that the viewer is a participant in, it seems to be a very interesting area to get into.

guy nouri: computer graphics consultant

Computer graphics has become a very important part of commercial production because, in many cases, it's faster and possibly cheaper, and it will get more and more that way. The effects that you can create and the kind of jobs that you can do with it are enormous. The only problem is, very few people in the industry understand what it is and how it works. At this point, I've become a computer graphics consultant because advertising agencies, production companies, and people in visual communications need to know what the potential of computer graphics is and how it can best be used.

I come from a fine arts background. I studied painting, filmmaking, photography, sculpture, and drawing for many years. I went to several different art schools. When I was at Princeton, I ran into this thing called computer graphics. Because it was another way of making images, I wanted to find out what it was about. So I took a class and was amazed at what was happening. Suddenly there seemed to be a whole new way of making images and a whole new genre of visual phenomena inside of this machine. After that, I went out to Xerox Parc in California, and by coincidence, ran into a friend and ended up working with him there on an informal basis doing animation. Then a period of time passed, and I came back to New York, where I started to get involved with it very seriously. There was no place to find out about computer graphics, so I did it all on the phone and by walking around and talking to people. I managed to learn enough to write some articles, which were popular, and I wound up creating and editing a magazine that was also successful. I went on from there to consult and also to produce some software.

I consult for advertising agencies. Usually, they want to know how much it will cost to get an effect and where the best place is to get that effect done. They don't know, they're at a loss. In many cases, they don't know the difference between slit scan and general motion graphics. When you start introducing something as complex as computer-generated graphics into the picture, they really get lost. They don't know whether one technique is more expensive. They don't know what the trade-offs are. They need to have their hand held. That's what I do. I hold hands. Frankly, there's been an enormous amount of reticence because the people in the advertising world are scared to death of what they don't know. If there's something they don't know, chances are they want to pretend it's not there, rather than to learn about it. But things are changing because their clients are demanding computer graphics more and more. As a result, they need to be informed.

I break computer graphics down into what I call the "MAD" three, which is motion control, analogue, and digital. Most people are familiar with motion control because it's all the same techniques of film animation graphics, except now the computer controls the activity of the camera, which just improves the efficiency of those processes. In motion control, all of the artwork and image making takes place outside of the computer. The computer is essentially being a "clerk" in keeping track of camera movements and timings. In analogue and digital, the image is manipulated inside the computer. In digital, it's actually generated inside the computer as well.

You don't have to be an animator to work with computer animation, but you have to know what you want. You have to have vision and creative talent. I know the very rudiments of animation, but I'm not an expert by any means. It's a vast field. All the conventional animation techniques apply, but there's a whole new set of techniques and styles that are possible, too. People see a technique and like it and want to work with it. They don't realize that there are a number of other techniques to work with as well. They're unaware of what the full potential is. In some cases, there are art directors who are willing to admit that they don't know. They ask questions, and they want to find out what they can do and how to best do it. That's when you begin to discuss what the trade-offs are. Sometimes to do an effect, you'd be better off using traditional methods, whereas sometimes you'd be far better off using computer techniques.

And inside of using computer techniques, some are more cost-effective than others. To know that, you have to understand how the machine works, what the programming is, and how the various capacities can be used.

I've been around for a while. I've been published in some magazines. I do a lot of lecturing and seminars—at least two or three a month. That gets me around. I wind up traveling to conferences. I prefer remaining independent from any particular production company. Every company has specific hardware and specific software. What they can produce is limited to the capabilities of their hardware, their software, and of course, the people who are running it, and what they are capable of from a creative and technical standpoint. The best thing I've found is to remain independent in order to work with all the companies, rather than to limit myself to any one set of possibilities.

Regarding the future of animation in the light of the advent of computers, I feel that, first of all, all of the things that can be replaced by the computer will be replaced by the computer, such as inking, painting, in-betweening, as well as a lot of the so-called special effects such as dissolves, wipes, and so on. They can all be done far more efficiently and economically by the computer. That will all be replaced probably within the next five, and certainly within the next 10, years. Inkers and painters will simply be out of business.

The second thing is that people are fascinated by this kind of imagery, because it has a way of grabbing the left and right sides of the brain simultaneously. It's intuitive and very strongly visual, and also, because of the mathematical origins, it appeals to logic. It has enormous precision as well. It's very captivating. People like this imagery. They want to be involved with it more and more. They want to use it. Live action will never disappear, but it will probably always be combined with some kind of computer-generated effect, background, or prop. It only seems to make sense. There's a whole new variety of images that have hardly been explored. They can be very powerful means of presenting a story or a message. You can simulate an actor in three dimensions, fully colored and shaded. That will be interesting, but it's not going to replace live action. It may have different applications. My feeling is that it will always be a combination. I'd like to see a one-on-one combination, where you have a live-action scene in direct composite with a computer scene, so that you have mixed realities. Where one picks up and the other leaves off would be completely indistinguishable. To me, it would be very magical, very powerful. And it's not far off now.

Three skills are useful in working with computer graphics. The first is an understanding of video and film making—f-stops, focus, shooting, editing, labs, and opticals. Second, you should have graphics skills. It's important that you have imagination and that you're creative with visual ideas. And last, you need an understanding of, if not some ability, in programming and the workings of the machinery, just so that you know what's going on in there, and more important, so that you're aware of what the possibilities are. That's essential, although it may be the last thing that people want to learn. But when they do learn about it, they start thinking in an entirely different way.

Let's take animatics as an example. That's something that can be done by the computer very easily, more effectively and quickly. Right now, there are one or two advertising agencies that have electronic storyboard generation. Instead of creating an animatic by moving pieces of cardboard around under a video camera, you can create the images on the computer, you can animate them on the computer, you can adjust them on the computer. You actually come up with something a little bit better than an animatic. You come up with something that's a lot closer to the final product and that is more accurate for testing purposes. If someone doesn't like a certain color or shape or position, you can go back and reset the numbers to solve that particular problem, rather than remaking the art and reshooting the whole thing. Then when you go into final production, you can just continue working from the original draft. You don't have to start from scratch. You can develop the image further right on the machine. You may start out with a sketch for the storyboard. Then, for the final, you can recall that sketch and add in more detail and color and rendering. There's no reason why an advertising agency, although they resist the notion of having any production in-house, couldn't have a system that could do down-and-dirty, quick animation right there on the spot. They could turn a commercial around in a matter of days, from storyboard to broadcast. That's something that I've been writing and talking to people about for a couple of years. They're interested in the idea, but they're still a little slow to get into it, partially due to the cost of the systems, which can range from $30,000 up to $250,000. And again, it's the hesitancy about what they don't know.

The animation union is quite friendly toward computer animation. The people who do computer animation have very little to do with the people who do conventional animation, because the techniques are so different. They're similar in that you create frames and put them together in succession. But the skills involved to do this are very different. Perhaps the computer animators don't belong in the Screen Cartoonists Guild. But at the same time, the union recognizes that their people are going to have to update if they're going to stay in business. So, instead of antagonism, which existed for a while, there seems to be a spirit of cooperation. Jack Harrell, president of the union in New York, has been very instrumental in bringing about those good feelings. At this point, I'm conducting seminars in computer animation for members of the union. I think a lot of good will come out of it for both parties.

Computer animation is new. It's at best 10 to 20 years old. People don't know what it is. It's quite apparent from how computers have affected every other segment of commercial existence that they are going to be an intrinsic part of the animation process. The computer is going to be THE TOOL when it comes to advertising, graphics, special effects, and visual communications. People need to learn about it. It's not so difficult. Maybe it involves a couple of weeks of training, and then people can begin to really work with the medium. So all I can say is, "Get on with it!"

epilogue: march 1984

Shortly after the preceding interview, Guy Nouri co-founded Interactive Picture Systems, Inc., with his partner, Eric Podietz. Their first product was PAINT, created for the Capital Children's Museum in Washington, D.C. PAINT is one of the earliest painting systems for personal computers and is currently being distributed by Atari, Inc.

Their next product was MOVIE MAKER™, a real time computer animation system that operates on the home computer and requires absolutely no programming knowledge. A full discussion of MOVIE MAKER™ can be found in Chapter 1 on page 31 under the section covering Computer Animation. MOVIE MAKER™ has received nationwide press and acclaim and is considered an unrivalled tool for creating computer cartoons.

With Guy Nouri as its President, IPS has rapidly grown to employ 15 full-time employees and a host of other free-lance people. The IPS team includes not only programmers, but artists, animators, musicians, and a group of specialists in the fields of their products. Currently, IPS is developing software for various publishers, and it is recognized as one of the leading software development companies in the personal computer industry.

george mc innis: animation production company owner

I am the president and founder of Image Factory. I am a designer/director and coordinator, also two-thirds businessman. I'm more of an entrepreneur than I am a designer today. I think the creative sense is extremely important, but to maintain a successful business, or I should say, to strive for a successful business, you have to be pretty cunning in this kind of market, because everybody wants a lot for nothing. It's very difficult. You have to be able to position yourself

strongly against a lot of adverse forces. It's quite different from being a heart surgeon or a lawyer. For us, there are no prescriptions. Each solution is a creation in itself. It's got its own set of problems. Our task as a design group is to solve those problems. There's no given time element to finding that solution. It may come at the eleventh hour, or it may begin in the first five minutes. Sometimes you go through an entire production without finding the proper solution until you finish and do it again. It's a difficult business.

The structure of the American economy, the guiding light of liberty's torch, even today, is that this is a land of opportunity, that an independent person can create his or her own business. My role is the execution of that principle.

When you put personal viewpoint and aesthetics into a commercial environment, you have to have the finances to support it. Either you are publicly funded, privately funded, or you have your own business. I've tried to construct a firm power structure inside an art-producing organization to give the opportunity of expression to my staff.

In my own case, as senior person in a growing group of artists, I spend a lot of energy securing business to keep my people working. I've taken a position of denial as an artist for a long time now. Occasionally I regret not being able to sit down at the drawing table myself. I miss it a great deal.

I've set up my company as more or less an installation, and in that installation are 15 or 20 people who are constructive and talented individuals working together. We have the company broken down into creative, technical, and management areas. I am responsible for assigning and distributing the work, but not for how it's going to be approached. I cross-train people, so they are familiar with one another's roles. My job is the creative management of creative personalities. The management of drive, energy level, and egos is very much like combining the colors and textures of paint to have them work together in a satisfying composition.

My own work as a designer is somewhat indirect. I get an idea, and I usually project it verbally and roughly sketched out to other persons. I tell them to go in that direction. There's a departure point at which I allow them to assume the idea as their own. Once they do that, I criticize it from there on out through the production. I find that in order to expand and develop new talent, I have to foster ego. I also have to disassociate myself from my own ego to avoid any possessiveness about ideas. We all benefit from it when it's finished.

Another of my functions is to maintain control between the client and my staff. Often, clients aren't willing to take risks on something new that they can't previsualize. They want to feel secure in that they know what they're getting. Our job is to give the client something of value. We try to come up with new and different solutions, so we have to guide the client to our way of thinking about his design problem and to our approach to producing it.

I started as a painter. After getting a few jobs doing paste-ups and mechanicals, interest was sparked in me for commercial graphics. I went to the School for the Visual Arts, taking courses in media and advertising for three years. After I graduated, I started working for a design firm in publishing, where I became art director of a monthly magazine. I continued from there into designing record and book covers, but very quickly, the standard format became limiting to me. I was making a lot of money, maybe 1000 or 2000 dollars a week, but I knew that this was not what I wanted to do. I wanted to create movement. I was interested in kinetic art. I'd been interested in films all my life. I was a television addict. I said to myself, "I know I can be really good at this. I'm not sure how I'm going to get to do it, but I am going to get to do it."

It was a hard decision to leave publishing, where I was comfortable and successful. But I had to make the break, because I wanted to work in television. I went back to school at night, where I met Roger Ferrata, who was a corporate art director at Metromedia. In fact, I intentionally took his class because he was the

corporate art director at Metromedia. I walked up to him and I said, "I really know that by the end of this class, you'll know that I'm the right person to work in that television station you have up on 67th Street." By the end of the course, he said to me, "You're absolutely right. How would you like a job?"

So I went to work for Metromedia, where I worked about 18 hours a day for very little money. Within two years, I was the tending art director. After that, I got a job as art director at ABC. Basically, they weren't using animation on air at that time. I talked them into doing 10-second animated station identification spots, rather than using held slides. My basic understanding of animation design and production comes from an on-the-job training situation. I created an animation format for ABC with different titles and program identifications on an ongoing basis. It was a very successful promotion, both in the sheer volume of animation produced each week, and also in its graphic quality.

My first encounter with doing something to please someone and having that person reject it was designing a feature title sequence for Lou Dorfsman at CBS. I was given the project to prove to Lou that I could in fact design animation graphics. I worked really hard on it, and he completely rejected it, and told me to let him show me how to do it right. I was really hurt, but it was probably the best learning experience I've ever had. I had to swallow my pride and readjust my thinking. It ignited in me an understanding of how to solve problems for different client situations. I got that from Lou Dorfsman—the greatest contribution that I've had to my career. He immediately hired me, and I worked with him for five years. It was a very strong working relationship. He taught me a tremendous amount, from how to manage people to how to deal with personalities, how to communicate ideas, how to have belief in the design that you stand for. He taught me how to become confident in my position as a designer.

The frustration of working as a designer and an animation director and having another company produce the work for me was what led me to form my own company. I was uncomfortable not having hands-on ability. You design everything, you lay it out, and then you send it out to somebody. It's like sending your shirts out to the laundry. You wait for them to come back, and then when you're getting dressed to go out, you discover there are no buttons on them. It was very difficult for me. It made me want to buy equipment, but CBS wouldn't hear of it. This was enough to make me want to leave CBS. In 1973, I started searching around the country for animation equipment, not having any idea how expensive it was. When I learned the very high cost of animation cameras, I realized that I was going to have to learn fast about banking and finance if I was going to be able to get involved with it at all. So I sat in my office at CBS for about a year and saved every dime I could. The next year, after getting very good banking advice from my bank, I took out a loan for half of the cost of the equipment. The other half of the money I invested myself. I had no money left to hire a camera operator, so I gave 40 percent of the company to a young cameraman named Mark Howard. He and I worked together for about three years, until Mark went out on his own. From there, I ran the company myself. I hired other people to do camera and production work, and I maintained design control. I started to develop Image Factory as it is today. As it has evolved, I've had to become more of an administrator and business manager.

I never wanted to do only animation. Our structure is such that we are a design shop that does corporate logos, letter heads, business cards, set design, as well as on-air graphics and television commercials. We also do corporate signage, convention displays, and even a building. We designed the art department for KABC, where we incorporated the personnel structure, the equipment, computer hardware and software for typography, and all of the interior and exterior space design.

It's hard to define a company like this. Most people look for specialists. It's taken me almost nine years to pull this all together. At first, we marketed ourselves separately to different clients. The design area would be presented in one avenue, the display area would be presented in another, and so on. We used different sales tactics for each function we served.

This diversification has allowed the company to survive. We couldn't have existed as solely an animation shop, because the pressures are too great. There aren't adequate deadlines or budgets. It's such a cost-competitive environment that it's hard to make a decent profit and maintain the high overhead we have.

In a tight economy, advertising clients want reality. What do you do if your clients want reality and you're producing cartoons? If you want to survive, you have to be able to swing with the times. The animation business is a very changeable one, a very hair-raising one. Especially if you have a lot of equipment and a large production staff. There are always whisperings of who's going out of business next.

This year, I'm launching the idea of a total design company for the first time, because I think the general commercial population is ready to accept it. In order to have some sense of security, you have to be multitalented and multifaceted, especially with the growing needs of communication today.

howard danelowitz: independent animator
balancing personal and commercial work

I was always interested in art and knew that I would be working in some art-related field. I went to Pratt Institute, where I took a general foundation art program. At that time I saw animated films that students had made there years ago that were really very impressive. In my sophomore year I took animation and live action. I liked them both equally, but I wanted to keep on drawing so animation won out. I started off animating with cutouts. I remember my teacher Sam Alexander, who's now head of Zeplin Productions. He was an excellent teacher. He was very pleased with my first film. It was Super-8. It was three minutes long, covering almost all techniques of animation, a whole smattering of what was possible. There's one scene where I did a moon rotating and flipping back and forth and he said, "Yes, this is what animation is!" It's when you destroy the illusion of a stage and things can move dimensionally any way you want. I tried to do that again and I was never quite able to. I realized that I had done something quite wonderfully by accident. About two years later I really felt I knew what I had done and I was able to control it.

So at that point, I was looking into California Institute of the Arts, where they would basically allow you to spend most of your time animating. At that point, that's what I wanted to do. I was studying with Jules Engel, a fine filmmaker and artist. There I made a few films—"Kaleidaform" and "The Funniest I Know is Mud Puddles," and I started on a long film called "Fields," that, as a matter of fact, is still going on right now. I look at it as an endless film. It's interesting because right now I am involved in doing commercial work, but I can clearly say that the "Fields" film will go on maybe forever. I've set up the perimeters that it won't have sound and it will be endless textures of movement. I'm always finding more possibilities, whereas in commercial work, there's always a deadline. There's not the flexibility or freedom to have a project go on and evolve. Right there is a large distinction between the two.

When I graduated Cal Arts, I moved to Boston. I was working part time, and I made a film called "Headstream," and then started another film called "Inside Out." I don't think I had much sense of the market, that I was making the films for any particular market, other than I felt that I was in an independent area. In many ways, I was making filmmakers' films, films that filmmakers could really appreciate. From other people I was really getting the spectrum of responses, from, "I have no idea what you're doing" to "Well, it has a nice feeling about it."

I was working at a community center teaching kids filmmaking and gymnastics. I was only working three hours a day. I finally got a job in the evening working at Mass College of Art,

teaching animation in Continuing Education. At this time, I was living very inexpensively. I spent a lot of time working on my films and earning enough money to live and do my own work. Those were my goals: to go on making better and better films. I did enjoy teaching and wanted to keep that up.

When I moved to New York, I got a job teaching at Philadelphia College of Art, and soon after, started teaching at Pratt Institute. I finished making "Inside Out." I also began doing some commercial work.

The first commercial project I worked on was actually still in Boston at the Educational Development Center. I worked on a show called "Infinity Factory." By the time I moved to New York, I was doing some commercial work with Eric Durst, who had been a student with me at Cal Arts.

Accepting commercial work seemed inevitable from my standpoint. In many ways, it was very attractive to me. The work paid well—that was a large consideration. There was some room for experimentation, because I was working in techniques I'd never used before. There was also the time constraint. I was learning, and yet at the same time, because of the deadline and budget considerations, there was a limitation to the experimentation possible.

It also had to do with other people finding value in my work. One of the first jobs I got when I moved to New York was to do the animated credit sequence for Brian dePalma's film "Home Movies." I basically got the job by showing him my film "Inside Out." It is not a narrative film. There's a lot going on, and it's hard to follow, but Brian saw something in it that he thought would suit his movie. I really had my doubts. I was thinking that he probably wanted funny little animated caricatures of the actors, and I'm not a caricature artist. But when I met with Brian and my competitor for the job, Brian realized that I not only made my own artwork, but I filmed it as well, and therefore my budgets were fairly small. When I said that, his eyes lit up, and I got the job over my competitor. I realized that having gone to Cal Arts, and having made my own films, shot them, and created my own sound tracks, I had a lot of skills that were useful.

The piece came out very nicely. I borrowed the drawing style from "Inside Out." That was my first transition from noncommercial to commercial work. I also hired other people to work on the project—Tracy Kirschenbaum, Eric Durst, Phillip Burke, and other people to ink and paint. I really saw that I enjoyed directing very much, and as a matter of fact, would like to spend more of my time directing. I found that I was good at getting other people to work together toward a common goal.

"Inside Out" seems to have been largely responsible for other noncommercial things as well. I received a grant from the New York Arts Council to make a film called "Lady Tree," which I'm working on right now. The grant was for $10,000. I had to apply for that grant through an organization, so I applied through Community Environments and proposed a project that they liked concerning the environment. They took 10% off the top for their bookkeeping work. The $9000 was left to carry out the film. In the meantime, I received a $20,000 grant from the American Film Institute, which I added to the production of "Lady Tree." AFI grants are largely based on past work, although they do look over the project you've proposed. I feel "Inside Out" was again responsible for my getting this grant (a very good feeling).

I've been working on "Lady Tree" for about two years, to the point where I find that I don't want to spend all of my time animating, so I've hired other people to work on the film. I'm finding different ways of working with other people on a piece that is basically noncommercial. That may not be an accurate description, however. Before starting the piece, I consulted with several organizations to talk about the film as a children's film, and as a children's book. I think it has large possibilities that way.

Sometimes people ask me, "What kind of returns do you get from 'Inside Out'? You

spend two years making a film. What happens to it? Is it shown? Do you receive any money for it?" These are important questions, especially if you want to earn a living doing your work. I actually have received monetary rewards from film festivals and payments from screening the film at theaters like Film Forum in New York, Center Screen in Cambridge, and others. But it's very minimal. You certainly don't earn a living from that, and you don't earn a living from having your work distributed. My work is distributed by the Museum of Modern Art, which has a certain prestige that helps you to get certain things. But, in itself, I don't earn much money. My works are also distributed by Picture Start, but again, the returns are minimal. Now my feelings are a little different, finishing "Lady Tree," in which I am even more aware of the marketplace. Before I even start the new film, I really want to get an idea of who will see this film, where it will be shown, what kind of audience it will have, and how long it should be. Do I want to make a short to show producers to raise money for a longer film? What are the possibilities of the cable market? Rather than just to make a film and hope it's going to get out there somehow, I want to take some responsibility for this up front. That's definitely what had happened to me previously. There was a feeling of "I love doing this work. I want to go on, and maybe something will happen." It was very passive. Whereas, with the high cost of living in New York, putting my own money into my films, demanding more of myself, and employing other people, things are less apt to be hit or miss. My own business sense has been developed by working on commercial projects.

You can live a very solitary life as an independent animator. You can literally be in a room all by yourself for many months at a time, making a film and shooting it in that same room if you have a camera there, and then putting it out in the world and hoping it will be seen. My idea has been more and more to collaborate with other people in order not to become isolated in the process, to feed ideas off each other. Fortunately, I haven't gotten to the place, and hope I never do get to the place, where I'm exhausted by working with other people. I do talk to people who have done commercial work only and worked only with other people, and they feel they're always compromising and never doing what they really want to do. I don't feel like that's my case. Perhaps it will happen at some point, and if it does, I'll have to make certain decisions. But that's not happening right now.

I want to talk a little bit about teaching and how that fits into the scheme of things. Many independent animators at one point or another do teach, because it's a way of earning a living and, at the same time, continuing to do your work, talking to people about your work, and getting feedback about it. I've found that my direction in teaching has been actually becoming a little more conservative. I encourage people to try a lot of different things, but I also find it important for people to acquire marketable skills so that they aren't lost when they finish school. When I went to school in the early 70s I had very little idea of how what I learned was going to fit into the scheme of the bigger world. Today, students want to know, "What can I do with these skills I'm learning? How can I get a job?" So basically, not only do we concentrate on learning different kinds of animation, but also on compiling some sort of reel to show people when the students get out of school, so they can get jobs. I do think it's important to be able to work in animation if you like animating. I think you can find the right setup for yourself, because there's a whole spectrum of commercial places. You may work in a place where you feel like you're just part of an assembly line, whereas in another place, you may feel that you're really animating and adding to the overall piece. I feel that's really fine.

At both schools I've taught at in the past few years, the chairpeople have clearly let it be known to the faculty that they did not want the departments known as places where students "do their own thing." They want the students to have very clear-cut skills and to be trained to move out into the marketplace. As a matter of fact, a new teacher was hired whose background is solely commercial work. This seems to be a prevailing attitude in schools today and a good indication of what we'll be seeing in stu-

dents that are coming out of schools today. A part of me is a little saddened by that.

I no longer separate my personal work from my commercial work. When I see good animation, whether it be commercial or noncommercial, there it is. It's good stuff. It may occur to me that there's this really wonderful movement and they're selling deodorant, but it's the animation that reads strongly to me no matter what form it's in. At one point, I think I did have a bias against commercial work. I felt that the most wonderful thing in the world was doing your own work. I still see that as wonderful, but I think your own work can be more accessible and still be your own work. Commercial work does come out more to the public. As I said, I've become very wary of isolating myself and my work. It's very difficult for me to anticipate working on a project right now if I will be working for long periods of time completely alone. Even though I do do that, I try to devise projects in which that doesn't have to happen a lot. When I graduated from school, there were a lot of people who came out of places like Harvard, School for the Visual Arts, Cal Arts, Pratt, Parsons, and other places, who had been doing experimental animation, graduated, and continued doing it. I think a lot of it has to do with age. You get older, and you start thinking, "Well, where do I go from here?" I think that was a big question for me. I think it happened in a natural way that I started gravitating a little more toward commercial animation. Now it's at the point where it doesn't get in the way of my independent work. I used to say, "I'm working on a personal film," and I had a friend who did commercial work who really resented that. I think she had the image of me hovering over my little film. I think I started getting that image a little bit, that I was hovering over my little whatever, and that somehow I was very little compared to the rest of the world. Somewhere I'd thought I was much larger. As you get older, you get more of a perspective of how you fit into the overall scheme of things. You're not as threatened to find out you're not as big as you thought you were. This is true of other people I went to school with, who were at that time doing only independent work, and who have now become

138

more attached to the commercial world. I think it's an inevitable evolution.

However, I think we may be seeing less personal animation as a result of this changing attitude. I think it has to do with people trying to earn livings and finding out that grants do not support living expenses as well as film expenses. Out of necessity, people have not had the luxury to make their own films. It is a loss. It has to do with the economy, too. There are fewer grants. I was very fortunate to have gotten this grant. But it's interesting that only half as many people applied this year as in the past. I think people are getting scared and thinking that this isn't the way to go in the future. How can you plan a future of grants? There will always be people who make their own films. It will always be a difficult path. But now that more independent animators are working in the industry, we can hope that the industry films will get better.

Throughout this interview, I feel as if I've been trying to define exactly what an independent animator is. When you're doing only personal work, it's easier to call yourself an independent animator because that's all you do. At one time, I did do that. But now I certainly feel that it's only a part of what I do.

As far as the future goes, I'd like to branch out in filmmaking. I've also become interested in computer animation. Basically, I want to continue to bring my work out in the world, in whichever form that's going to be.

**one and a half years later
december 21, 1983**

AN EPILOGUE
At the opening reception for "Lady Tree," the following press release, written by Marsha J. Lebby, was distributed. As indicated in its title LADY TREE BRANCHES OUT, it best captures the already-growing life of the film and my current activities.

"Having its premiere at the prestigious 1983 New York Film Festival, Howard Danelowitz's latest animation creation, "Lady Tree" will now tour with Armand Hammer Productions docudrama feature, "Backstage at the Kirov." Both events are rare in the world of animation. Only three animated shorts were selected from among scores submitted to the Film Festival's selection committee for screening at the exclusive New York event. Sadly, the days of a "movie" and a cartoon short are behind us.

"Producers of 'Backstage at the Kirov' chose to recapture that tradition by pairing their artistically-conceived ballet film with the equally artistic "Lady Tree." Noted for its sophistication of design and rich range of color, the animated short also boasts a haunting sound track by Academy Award winner Normand Roger. The charming, thought-provoking animation parable of Nature vs. the forces of urbanization drew applause at its film fest debut. In hopes of branching out still further, it will be entered in this year's Academy Award competition.

"Danelowitz (producer/director/designer and creative force behind his New York Animation company) is no stranger to awards, having garnered his share at both Filmex and the American Film Festival for "Inside Out." The versatile animator is no stranger to television, either, with shorts recently aired on both Showtime and Cinemax. Coming up will be directorial work on "Reading Rainbow"—the PBS children's program.

"'Lady Tree' represents one side of Danelowitz's efforts—work in commercials the other. Through the Harold Friedman Consortium, he has worked on a number of spots and recently did a stint at R.O. Blechman's Ink Tank. Future work will encompass a mix of both worlds. The company can handle virtually any animation style, drawn or computer-generated. Like Lady Tree herself, New York Animation, having put down its roots, will be around for a long time to come."

conclusion

From its origins in the late nineteenth century, the evolution of animation has been rooted in a fascination with technology and visual design. As much as technological advances have affected the design possibilities of animation, so has the exploration of new designs and animation techniques influenced the development of the equipment and technology used to create them.

In recent years, the graphic potential of the computer has evolved to a point where a whole new realm of animation style and technique is possible. The area of computer animation is rapidly expanding, as designers and computer programmers find a common language. This interaction between designers and programmers promises the creation of animated imagery that has not yet been seen.

Besides its unique graphic style, the computer is also useful in assisting other animation techniques. Perhaps the computer will never replace hand-drawn cel animation, but in some cases, it can save time and work in the process by in-betweening or adding color. Some computers are able to provide testing of design and movement in real time, thereby eliminating the pencil test stage, and allowing for immediate adjustments of artwork and animation.

Computer-assisted cameras allow for precise control in shooting and combining various elements onto one final piece of film.

When used effectively, the computer can save time and money and free the artist to concentrate more of his energy on his ideas.

At this point, there are room and need for both computerized and noncomputerized animation techniques. The computer is an additional tool for the creation of animated images, and its advent should not be considered a threat to the other tools.

Although most animation is done on film, there are also video animation systems that allow for "single frame" shooting. Two such systems are Lyon-Lamb and Anivid. They are convenient tools for immediate pencil test results and other forms of real time experimentation. Analogue computer animation, that is, the distortion and manipulation of existing artwork by a computer, is output on videotape.

However, there is a subtle but noticeable difference in the texture and look of video animation as compared to film animation. It is important to be aware of this difference if the choice is made to work in video.

We have examined the various techniques and applications of animation. These are the animator's tools, and he must make conscious decisions about each and every one. To reiterate, the essential modules of animation are successive static images. From here, the choices begin, from the graphic material and style, to the lighting, the film stock, the camera's relationship to the subject, and the relation between sound and image. Furthermore, the animator is responsible for the quality of his prints, as well as the way his films are projected. He must learn about the illusion of movement created in animation, and the way in which his artwork will be perceived when projected in real time. He must acquire an understanding of the effect of the film's rhythm from sequence to sequence and from frame to frame.

The more the animator becomes familiar with the tools and techniques of animation, the better he will be able to use them to his own advantage, rather than working against or in spite of them. As he masters his tools, he will be able to make the films he wants to make. They are the equivalent of words to the poet or stone to the sculptor. The animator's mastery of his tools will enable him to affect his audience as he desires.

In other words, an animator must make choices in his work to evolve the language of animation. The more he works, the more he will understand how his images are perceived by his audience. He will learn how to affect the viewer's conscious involvement, as well as his subconscious perceptions as he watches the film.

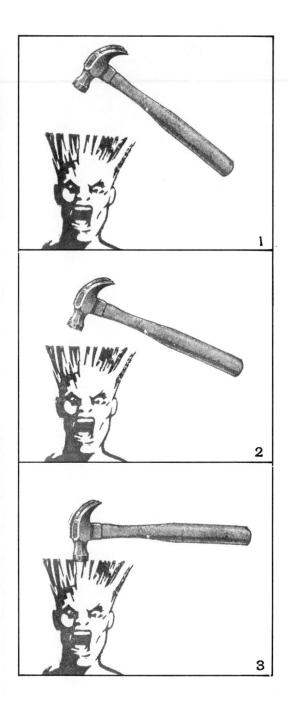

In every film, there is the potential for the unique use of the language of animation. It is important that the animator be conscious of the choice of his language, and be consistent with its use throughout the film. The language, the grammar, and the structure of the film should be established at its beginning, so that the viewer will be able to adjust his perceptions while watching the film.

Animation is a medium that has invention inherent in it. Every frame is a new creation, and the tools used in the creation of each frame are constantly open to choice and change. At the same time, it is a very slow and sometimes tedious process. The making of an animated film involves this unlikely combination of meticulous work and unlimited creative decision. It is a medium that has always been, and continues to be, ripe for exploration. Animation is truly a vehicle for inspiration and imagination.

glossary

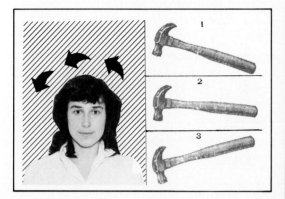

aerial image animation The combination of live action and top-lit animation with only one pass of the film through the camera. The live action is rear-projected and focused onto a plane below that of the top-lit animation.

analogue computer animation A computer graphics system that enables the manipulation of existing artwork on videotape. The analogue signal is understood by the computer as continuous data.

animatic A simplified rendition of a television commercial, usually shot from preliminary drawings of each scene on videotape. The animatic is used to test the effectiveness of the concept of the commercial.

animation stand An assembly that holds the camera securely while the artwork is being shot frame by frame.

animator In the animation production, the person who brings the designs and characters to life through animation.

answer print The film print on which the sound and picture are composited as one piece of film.

anticipation The small, preliminary action that leads in to the major animated action. For example, the arm pulling back before it launches forward in a punch.

aperture The rectangular opening in the gate of the camera through which light passes to expose the film frame that is in front of it.

ASA In the United States, the standard scale of measuring a film's sensitivity to light, referred to as the speed of the film. The more sensitive the film, the higher the ASA, and the faster the film. The equivalent European scale is DIN.

aspect ratio The dimensions of the rectangular area framed by the camera lens. The standard 16 mm film frame has an aspect ratio of 1.376 to 1, width to height.

back-lit animation Animation artwork that is designed to be lit from underneath when being filmed. Combinations of Kodaliths and colored gels are typically shot back-lit.

bi-packing The combination of multiple film elements in the camera. This technique requires a bi-pack magazine that allows the loading of two pieces of film at a time.

blow-up The reprinting of a smaller format film stock onto a larger format stock.

cable release A flexible metal rod that triggers the shutter release from a distance of several feet, eliminating the need to push the trigger by hand.

camera original/camera negative The film that is run through the camera, exposed, and processed.

cel Clear sheets of cellulose acetate on which cel animation artwork is created on multiple levels. Generally, animation cels are 10.5" by 13" and 0.005" thick.

cel animation The use of multiple levels of animation created on several layers of transparent acetate cels. When only part of a scene is to be animated and the rest of it remains constant, it is not necessary to redraw the whole drawing for each frame. By creating drawings on layers of cel, separate elements of a scene may be animated on separate levels.

checker In the animation production, the person who reviews the inked and painted cels before they are shot to ensure that all areas of color have been applied and that none of the cels is out of numerical order.

claws Small movable metal prongs in the gate area of a camera and projector that engage the sprocket holes of the film and pull it through the gate frame by frame.

closed session bid A bidders' information conference in which the advertising agency producer arranges individual appointments with the producers from each competing production company to discuss the job on a private basis.

collage animation The use of cutout, collaged shapes to create animation.

color correction Slight color adjustments made by the lab in the printing of the film. Also known as "timing."

CRI Color reversal internegative. An intermediate print off the camera original that is used in creating the final optical print.

cross-dissolve A film effect in which one image fades out as a new image fades in simultaneously. A cross-dissolve can be created as an optical effect or as a camera effect during filming of the artwork.

cycle A series of animation drawings that begin and end with the same position.

daylight film Film stock that is used in daylight. It is less sensitive to blue tones than indoor, or Tungsten, film.

depth of field The range of acceptable focus that the lens sees.

designer/director In the animation production, the creator of the visual design and production of a film, who works on the basis of the original storyboard.

digital computer animation A computer graphics system that generates and animates graphics. The digital signal is understood by the computer as discreet units of data.

digitization The assignment of a numerical value to each point of an image, indicating color or gray tone. Live-action footage can be digitized by a video scan and then combined indistinguishably with computer-generated imagery.

DIN The standard European scale of measuring a film's sensitivity to light. The equivalent of the ASA scale in the United States.

direct animation The process of frame-by-frame animation which is achieved during the filming process. It is often known as animating "under the camera," because the creation and manipulation from frame by frame occurs as the camera is shooting frame by frame. Examples are object animation, puppet animation, clay animation, and pinscreen animation.

drawn animation Animation created from successive drawings that change minutely from one to the next.

exposure sheets Frame-by-frame instructions given to the cameraman by the animator as to how the animation artwork is to be shot. They account for every layer of artwork, and indicate all changes in artwork and camera position for every frame.

f-stop The numerical measurement of the iris setting that determines the size of the aperture and the amount of light entering the camera and exposing the film. F-stops are calibrated on the lens from 1 to 1.4, 2, 2.8, 4, 5.6, 8, 11, 16, and 22. Each successive F-stop cuts the amount of light by exactly half.

fade in The gradual appearance of an image from black. A fade in can be created as an optical effect or as a camera effect during the filming of the artwork.

fade out The gradual disappearance of an image to black. A fade out can be created as an optical effect or as a camera effect during the filming of the artwork.

field guide The standard reference for the proper framing ratios of the artwork so they will match exactly the camera's aspect ratio.

fine cut The final, double-spliced, edited version of a film.

flip book A stack of separate images flipped by hand to create the illusion of movement and transformation. A form of camera-less animation.

focal length The measurement in millimeters of the lens indicating its angle of view. The lower the focal length, the wider the area framed by the lens.

format The size of the film stock, indicating the width and frame size. Format is measured in millimeters, and film stock is available in 8 mm and Super-8, 16 mm, 35 mm, and 70 mm.

frame One unit of film that holds a single image of a sequence. There are 24 frames per second when film is projected at normal speed. There are 40 16 mm frames and 16 35 mm frames in a foot of film.

freeze frame An optical effect in which one frame of an action is frozen in a held position.

gate The path in the camera in front of the lens through which the film travels.

gels Transparent colored sheets of acetate. By combining Kodaliths and various gels, and lighting them from underneath, a unique style of graphic animation is produced.

gimbal box A device rigged in the cutout area of the animation compound to allow for stop motion animation of small objects in three dimensions.

HI CON High contrast black and white film stock that produces an image that translates colors into either black or white, and minimizes gray tones.

illustrator In the animation production, the skilled artist who renders the visions and concepts of the designer/director, the polished storyboard, the character models, and the backgrounds for the animation, depending on the requirements of the job.

in-betweener In the animation production, the person who draws the sequence of frames between the animator's key drawings, following the animator's style of line, movement, and characterization.

incident light meter A light meter that

measures the amount of light that falls onto the subject.

inker In the animation production, a person who traces the animation drawings onto cels with ink.

inking The stage of the animation process in which the completed pencil animation drawings are traced with ink onto punched cels and broken into separate layers.

interlock The stage of editing in which the picture and sound have been fine cut, as two separate pieces of stock.

intermittent motion The mechanism in the camera and projector that allows film to move through at a constant rate and at the same time allows each frame to be retained in the gate for a fraction of a second.

intervalometer An auxiliary variable speed motor that can be attached to the camera to regulate the intervals at which each frame is exposed.

IP Interpositive. An intermediate print off the camera original that is used in creating the final optical print.

iris An adjustable mechanism at the back of the lens, close to the film plane, that regulates the amount of light coming into the camera.

kelvin color temperature scale The scale that measures the temperature of a light source. A 60-watt light bulb is 2800 degrees K; noontime sunlight is 5400 degrees K.

key frames The start and end positions of an animated movement. Drawn animation may be done from key frames if the action and timing are predetermined. The key frames, or "extremes," of each movement are drawn first. The length of time for the move determines the number of drawings that must be added in between to get from the first to the last position.

kodalith Artwork made on high-contrast film for backlit animation work. The image is clear and the rest of the frame is black. By combining Kodaliths and colored gels, and lighting them from underneath, a unique style of graphic animation can be produced.

light table A translucent drawing surface with a light source underneath. It enables the animator to see through the drawing he is working on to the drawings underneath for reference.

leader Sprocketed film stock that has no image or frame lines. Available in black, clear, or colors. It is generally used on the heads and tails of films to lead in and out of the picture. It can also be used in making camera-less animation. Black leader can be punched with holes, and its emulsion can be scratched off in various patterns. Clear leader can be painted with different colors and shapes. When such leader is projected, exciting animated rhythms and forms are produced.

matte box A device attached to the camera to hold positive and negative mattes between the camera and the artwork, to allow for different scenes to be exposed into different parts of the frame.

motion control The use of a computer to automate the operation of an animation stand for the creation of special effects and graphic animation.

multiple pass backlit motion graphics The technique of combining several backlit art elements onto one piece of film by multiple shooting runs.

negative film stock Film stock that results in a negative image when it is exposed and processed.

negative matte A piece of black material that is cut out to obscure a specific area of the film frame. Its opposite is the corresponding positive matte. Also, the high-contrast film of the area obscured by the negative matte.

nonreflex viewing system A camera system in which a separate viewing mechanism, or viewfinder, must be used to determine what the lens is framing. Such systems must compensate for the problem of parallax.

opaquer In the animation production, a person who applies the paint to the inked animation cels. Also called "painter."

opaquing The stage of the animation process in which the paint is applied to the inked cels. Special paints, created to adhere to acetate without cracking or flaking, are applied to the back sides of the cels one color at a time.

open session bid A bidders' information conference in which producers from each competing production company are called into the advertising agency at the same time to discuss the job.

optical printing The precise and controlled rephotography of one piece of film onto another.

optical track The version of the sound track that is a very thin photographic line that runs along the edge of the film beside the image and changes in pattern and width. The optical track is analyzed by a light beam in the sound head of the projector and converted into sound waves.

overlapping action The movement of different parts of an animated character's body, clothing, and accessories at different rates of speed, all relating to the main activity.

pan A horizontal, vertical, or diagonal camera move along the artwork.

pantograph A specially designed platform with a movable pointer that is attached to the side of the animation compound and facilitates the execution of complex camera movements over one image.

parallax The slight difference between what the lens sees and what the viewfinder sees in a nonreflex camera.

pegbar A thin piece of metal with three pegs that correspond to the three registration holes punched along the edge of the animation paper. By placing each sheet of paper on the pegbar while the animation drawings are being made, and then while they are being shot, the sequence of drawings will remain in registration with each other.

pencil test The film test of the animation that is drawn with pencil on paper. The pencil test is screened to preview and adjust the pencil animation before the final artwork is created.

persistence of vision The ability of the human retina to retain a visual image for approximately 1/10 of a second.

PHI phenomenon The perceptual trait that is the conceptual equivalent of persistence of vision. It enables us to understand a series of rapidly changing sequential still images as connected and related.

photo animation The creation of animation by camera moves over photographs. Also, the use of sequential still photographs to create an animated sequence. Live-action film can be printed frame by frame as black and white photographs. These photo sequences can be hand-painted, cut up, and mounted on registered cels. The images can then be incorporated into any desired background and rephotographed on the animation stand.

pinscreen A large white board through which many thousands of thin pins are inserted. By changing the lengths and depths of the pins in the board, variations in shading from black to white are created. These can be manipulated into shapes and forms that can be animated frame by frame.

platen The piece of optically corrected glass that is placed over the layers of cels to keep them flat while they are being filmed.

positive matte A piece of black material that is cut out to reveal only a specific area of the film frame. Its opposite is the corresponding negative

148

matte. Also, the high-contrast film of the area revealed by the positive matte.

post-flashing A laboratory process in which unprocessed film is exposed to light briefly before it is developed in an attempt to bring up a low-light situation.

pre-flashing A process in which unexposed raw stock is exposed to light briefly before it is shot in an attempt to bring up a low-light situation.

pressure plate The metal plate that holds the film firmly against the gate so that it travels smoothly.

producer The overall supervisor, organizer, and coordinator of a film production; the liaison between the advertising agency and the production staff.

pushing A laboratory process in which the film is developed longer than normal to bring out as much of the image as possible in a potentially underexposed picture.

raster graphics A display of computer imagery that presents the image as individual points that are combined to create a given graphic.

reduction The reprinting of a larger format film stock onto a smaller format stock.

reflective light meter A light meter that measures the amount of light reflected off the subject.

reflex viewing system A camera feature that, by means of mirrors, enables the camera operator to see directly through the lens.

registration The technique of assuring that corresponding points on two sequential frames of animation artwork bear the correct relationship to each other. The standard registration system uses three holes punched along the top of each sheet of paper. These holes correspond to three pegs on a pegbar onto which the punched paper is placed. The holes and the pegs

are outside of the field of artwork that the camera will shoot. There is a matching pegbar on the animation stand, so that the drawings can be aligned precisely as they were drawn when they are being shot.

reversal film stock Film stock that results in a positive image when it is exposed and processed.

rotoscoping The use of live action film as a reference standard in the creation of animation artwork.

rough cut The first step in editing a film, in which the shots are single spliced together in sequential order, leaving extra footage at the head and tail of each shot.

secondary motion In an animated gesture, the follow-up movement to the main action.

shutter A semicircular metal disk located between the aperture and the film, which rotates once per frame, allowing light to enter the aperture and expose the film.

sinex test A single frame exposure test made by shooting one frame for each F-stop and changing the setting at regulated intervals. Also known as "wedge test."

slit scan A special effects technique in which the artwork is shot through a slit or series of slits onto one frame of film at a time, as the camera moves in complex paths.

sound mix The stage of the film production during which individual sounds are equalized and balanced, and multiple sound tracks are combined onto one final mixed track.

spec sheet The advertising agency's delineation of the specific requirements for a commercial film production.

spot A television commercial.

sprockets Small holes running along the edges of film stock that are engaged by pins, or "claws," in the camera or projector to facilitate threading.

squash and stretch The technique of exaggeration of a gesture in animation. The distortion given to a normal reaction to make it more forceful.

storyboard Preliminary sketches of the action of a film in sequential order. The storyboard serves as the initial description of the animation and is necessary in discussion and planning of the production.

straight ahead animation Animation whose direction evolves as it is being drawn frame by frame.

streak A trail of translucent light that is left by an object or a work. It is created by zooming on a piece of backlit artwork with the shutter held open on each frame for the full length of the zoom.

superimposition The combination of two separate sequences of action on a single piece of film. One sequence is filmed, the film is rewound back to the starting frame, and the second sequence is then exposed, or "superimposed" over it.

sync The synchronous relationship between film sound and image.

timing Slight color adjustments made by the lab in the printing of the film. Also known as "color correction."

top-lit animation Animation artwork that is lit from above when being filmed. Drawings and animation cels are generally shot top-lit.

traveling mattes Hand-painted or cutout black mattes that correspond to a live or animated form as it moves and changes frame by frame. Traveling mattes are used to combine several separate images onto one piece of film as a single scene.

tungsten film Film stock used with artificial light sources. It is less sensitive to reds and oranges than daylight film.

variable shutter A second independent shutter that is regulated separately from the main shutter. It can be closed down or opened up gradually to create in-camera fades and dissolves.

vector graphics A display of computer imagery that presents forms as a series of smooth lines drawn on the screen from point to point.

wedge test A single-frame exposure test made by shooting one frame for each F-stop and changing the setting at regulated intervals. Also known as "sinex test."

wire frame The skeletal form of an image created by a vector graphics display.

workprint A print made from the camera original and used for screening and editing work, so that the original can remain untouched and undamaged.

xerox animation The use of a Copyflo machine to Xerox live-action film frame by frame onto a roll of paper. These images can then be used as animation artwork.

zoom A camera move toward or away from the subject.

zoom lens A lens that offers a range of focal lengths in one lens.

bibliography

animation: production and technique

Blair, Preston, Animation: Learn How to Draw Animated Cartoons. Laguna Beach, CA: Foster, 1949.

Eastman Kodak Company. Basic Tilting and Animation for Motion Pictures. 2nd edition, Publications S-21. Rochester, NY, 1976.

Eastman Kodak Company. The World of Animation. Publication S-35. Rochester, NY.

Fielding, Raymond. The Technique of Special Effects Cinematography. New York: Hastings House, 1969.

Halas, John. Computer Animation. New York: Hastings House, 1974.

Halas, John, and Bob Privett. How to Cartoon. London and New York: Focal Press, 1958.

Halas, John, and Harold Whitaker. Timing for Animation. Woburn, MA: Focal Press, 1981.

Laybourne, Kit. The Animation Book. New York: Crown Publishers, 1979.

Levitan, Eli L. Animation Techniques and Commercial Film Production. New York: Reinhold Publishing Company, 1962.

Madsen, Roy P. Animated Film: Concepts, Methods, Uses. New York: Interland, 1969.

Perisic, Zoran. The Animation Stand. New York: Hastings House, 1976.

Perisic, Zoran. Special Optical Effects. Woburn, MA: Focal Press, 1980.

Perlman, Herman. Animated Cartooning. Washington, DC: The Cartoonimator Company, 1946.

Wilkie, Bernard. Creating Special Effects for TV and Film. Woburn, MA: Focal Press, 1977.

152 | **animation: history and theory**

Ceram, C.W. Archaeology of the Cinema. New York: Harcourt, Brace, and World, 1965.

Field, Robert. The Art of Walt Disney. New York: Macmillan Company, 1942.

Film Comment. The Hollywood Cartoon. New York: The Film Society of Lincoln Center, Jan.-Feb., 1975.

Halas, John, and Roger Manvell. The Technique of Film Animation. New York: Hastings House, 1968.

Hepworth, Cecil. Animated Photography: The ABC of The Cinematograph. New York: Arno Press, 1970.

Hoffer, Thomas. Animation: A Reference Guide. Westport, CT: Greenwood Press, 1981.

Holloway, Ronald. Z is for Zagreb. London: The Tantivy Press, 1972.

Kriegsman, Sali Ann, and Alex Ward. AFI Report: Animation. Washington, DC: American Film Institute, Vol. 5, No. 2, Summer 1974.

Maltin, Leonard. The Disney Films. New York: Crown. 1973.

Maltin, Leonard. Of Mice and Magic: A History of American Animated Cartoons. New York: Plume, 1980.

Manvell, Roger. The Animated Film. New York: Hastings House, 1955.

Muybridge, Eadweard. Animals in Motion. New York: Dover, 1955.

Muybridge, Eadweard. The Human Figure in Motion. New York: Dover, 1955.

Russett, Robert, and Cecile Starr. Experimental Animation: An Illustrated Anthology. New York: Van Nostrand Reinhold Company, 1976.

Schickel, Richard. The Disney Version. New York: Simon and Schuster, 1968.

Stephenson, Ralph. The Animated Film. New York: A.S. Barnes and Company, 1973.

TRICKFILM/Chicago '80. Chicago: Film Center, School of the Art Institute of Chicago. 1980.

film: production and theory

Bresson, Robert. Notes on Cinematography. New York: Urizen Books, 1975.

Curtis, David. Experimental Cinema. New York: Universe Books, 1971.

Eastman Kodak Company. The Selection and Use of Kodak and Eastman Motion Picture Films. Publication H-1. Rochester, NY.

Kracauer, Siegfried. Theory of Film. New York: Oxford University Press, 1960.

Lawder, Standish. The Cubist Cinema. New York: New York University Press, 1975.

Lipton, Lenny. Independent Filmmaking. San Francisco: Straight Arrow Books, 1972.

Malkiewicz, Kris. Cinematography: A Guide for Filmmakers and Film Teachers. New York: Van Nostrand Reinhold, 1973.

Munsterberg, Hugo. The Film: A Psychological Study. New York: Dover, 1970 (first published by D. Appleton and Company, NY, in 1915).

Sitney, P. Adams. Film Culture Reader. New York: Praeger Publishers, 1970.

Sitney, P. Adams. Visionary Film. New York: Oxford University Press, 1974.

Index